Living the Spiritually Balanced Life

Ray S. Anderson

Baker Books

A Division of Baker Book House Co
Grand Rapids, Michigan 49516

Published by Baker Books
a division of Baker Book House Company
P.O. Box 6287, Grand Rapids, MI 49516-6287

Printed in the United States of America

Library of Congress Cataloging-in-Publication Data

Anderson, Ray Sherman.
    Living the spiritually balanced life / Ray S. Anderson.
        p.   cm.
    Includes bibliographical references.
    ISBN 0-8010-5803-1
    1. Virtues. 2. Spiritual life—Christianity. I. Title.
BV4630.A65   1998
241'.4—dc21   98-8101

For current information about all releases from Baker Book House, visit our web site:
                    http://www.bakerbooks.com

Contents

Contents

6/11/99

To our granddaughter Beth, in her graduation from High School.

We hope, the reading of this book, helps you to know yourself better, and guide you to a deeper understanding.

With much love,

Grandpa and Grandma

Preface

Preface

The fruit of the Spirit is love, joy, peace, patience, kindness, generosity, faithfulness, gentleness, and self-control. There is no law against such things.

Galatians 5:22–23

Virtues are the character qualities we admire in other people. We value these qualities because we benefit from being close to people who have them, and we sense that they have achieved a quality of life toward which we aspire. While Christians do not have a corner on virtue, the Bible makes it clear that God is the source and developer of all human virtue. So when the apostle Paul lists the fruit of the Spirit in the life of the believer, he is identifying the virtues we all recognize and value—love, joy, peace, patience, kindness, generosity, and so forth (Gal. 5:22–23).

We might reasonably expect to find these virtues consistently exhibited in the lives of religious people, but this is not always so. Quite the contrary, as Jesus himself discovered. Those in his day who were most scrupulous about practicing their religion were often the most lacking in the virtues of compassion, gentleness, and love, to name just a few. What drew people to Jesus was not the splendor of his divine visage but the extraordinary way in which he embodied and displayed human virtue.

As the Son of God, and thus the perfect human being, Jesus is the flawless expression of the image of God that the rest of us reflect so dimly. Merely being religious—following religion's rules, rituals, and regulations—cannot ensure quality of character. But Paul shows that when we are led by the Spirit of God, the character of Jesus becomes formed in our lives. The fruit of his Spirit gives evidence of our transformation from people with inhuman attitudes and actions to those with the virtues of true humanity. Spiritual maturity, or what I like to call spiritual fitness, is the mark of a person created in the divine image who, through divine grace, is effectively manifesting the God-like virtues of true humanity.

When Paul scolded the Christians in the church at Galatia, he assumed that they had "received the Spirit of Jesus" and therefore should bear the "fruit of the Spirit" (Gal. 5:22–23). This fruit is the expression of those spiritual qualities that make us more truly human. But for each quality that denotes the Spirit's fruit there is a corresponding "work of the flesh" that indicates a lack of spiritual maturity. The "works of the flesh" are inhuman and destructive to personal and social dignity and integrity. Having received the Spirit of Jesus, Paul argues, one should manifest the fruit of this Spirit not by religious behavior or creedal profession alone but by developing and practicing those qualities that lead to spiritual fitness. Spiritual fitness, like physical fitness, activates inner resources for healing, releases untapped energy, and produces a sense of personal well-being that contributes to the good of others. Where spiritual fitness or maturity is lacking, instead of honesty, there will be deception and shame; instead of compassion, there will be envy and hatred (5:19–21).

In this book I attempt to show that there are measurements on the scale of spiritual fitness that enable us to discern the precise meaning of bearing the fruit of the Spirit in our daily lives. Each chapter, therefore, probes one of the Christian virtues by exploring a key positive aspect while contrasting its corresponding negative side. My listing and treatment of the virtues is meant to be suggestive, not exhaustive. They are not listed in any particular order. Each of us possesses some and desires others.

Spiritual maturity, as the flowering of Christian virtues, is God's provision and promise for every Christian, through the indwelling power of the Holy Spirit. But the pathway to spiritual maturity is a rocky road with many pitfalls. It is filled with skewed perspectives and temptations to excess that can hamper or arrest our progress.

Every move toward spiritual maturity, therefore, requires discernment and balance. In fact, spiritual balance may be seen as the applied skill that leads to spiritual maturity. With each step taken, there is the reward of personal growth and divine blessing. The apostle Paul wisely instructed us to "work out our own salvation," but he knew we need God's help in that process. That is why I have called this book *Living the Spiritually Balanced Life.* I hope that in it you will find practical and biblical counsel for developing within yourself the virtues you admire in others.

1

Self-Control

Being Angry
without Losing Your Temper

Be angry but do not sin; do not let the sun go down on your anger.

Ephesians 4:26

"I don't like it when I get angry and lose control of myself," Jim confessed. "I'm always ashamed of myself later. But I have to admit that while I am venting my anger I feel good. It's strange. I feel a sense of exhilaration, a sense of power, as though I were on some kind of drug. Maybe I'm addicted to anger!"

The emotion of anger has a narcotic effect. Anger has a kick to it, both for the one who expresses it and for the person at the receiving end. It is the ultimate stimulant and an intravenous source of pleasure to placate narcissistic pain. There is no hurt so intense that anger cannot express it and no pain so personal that anger cannot caress it. Like

Jacob who wrestled with the angel of God, I will not let go of my anger until it blesses me, even though it leaves me lame and limping. Anger serves a purpose and will not be released until it has done its work. There are times when we are so angry that sympathy is intolerable and comfort seems cruel. The voice of reason is deaf to the logic of anger, for at the deepest level, anger is outrage against the perceived threat of extinction.

Anger is the mask put on the face of fear, the fear that comes with us through the birth passage to life on the planet. From the beginning, the human creature carries the burden of knowing that life and security can be lost.

Perhaps this is why the smallest infant can slip into a rage so virulent that any attempt to comfort produces further outrage. Anger in the newborn occurs so readily that one suspects it is a prenatal emotion. If the unborn self has a sense of apprehension and a feeling of impending violation to its dignity, this is quickly confirmed by the snip of a scissors and a slap to the behind, all the while being held upside down! The "cry of life" is, at the same time, a spasm of anger. It is not pretty, but it is perfect! For all our gratitude at having been born, it is clear that our entrance into the world is both undignified and humiliating. Someone needs to be forgiven for that! But there is more to follow.

To be born human is to be thrust into an arena where every feeling that gives pleasure is eventually met with disapproval or denial. In the beginning, the infant experiences being out of control as natural and good. Bodily functions, personal feelings, and exploratory movements are spontaneous and uninhibited; being out of control feels normal. Another judgment is made, however, by those responsible to socialize the child through fostering patterns of conformity. The first lesson is about to begin. Unfortunately, though, it does not appear that the human psyche at birth was wired to appreciate delayed gratification for the sake of future gain!

Learning to control one's feelings, functions, and future means coming under discipline. And, as the Bible tells us, "Discipline always seems painful rather than pleasant at the time" (Heb. 12:11). The text goes on to say, "but later it yields the peaceful fruit of righteousness to those who have been trained by it."

To be brought under discipline is to come up against resistance to our felt needs. To be brought under control is to have external forces restrict the freedom of internal drives. Whatever the moral good intended in such discipline, we sense that it is wrong to have limits set to the spontaneous reach for what feels good! The invasion of one's personal world of self-gratification is experienced as a kind of violence by the undeveloped moral instincts that defend the right to pleasure.

The feeling of anger usually carries with it some implied moral judgment. But in the first instance our moral sense focuses not on our conscience but on self-preservation. Initially, the emotion of anger is an inarticulate expression of moral outrage at that which threatens one's innate sense of well-being.

Such anger quickly goes awry. And uncontrolled anger makes the moral sense oblivious to all but one's own rights. Caught in the rhythmic spasms of inner rage, self-preservation becomes blind to its effect upon others. As seen from the outside, the person caught in the tornado of temper is clearly out of control. But to the angry person, the only power sufficient to retain control over a world slipping from his grasp is furious anger.

At this point, the angry person knows that he is out of control and that he has grossly misused any underlying moral passion. This is why, in an adult, an explosion of temper usually results in feelings of shame when it has subsided. One suspects that it has the same effect on children, though shame as a concept lies hidden within the inarticulate world of the child bruised by its own surrender to a passion beyond its understanding. The shame is there, however, and is carried over into adulthood as a malignant tumor lodged in the muscle of self-esteem.

There is no virtue in uncontrolled anger, as the Bible indicates. "Let everyone be quick to listen, slow to speak, slow to anger; for your anger does not produce God's righteousness" (James 1:19–20). In relation to anger, self-control is the virtue of experiencing feelings of anger but not giving way to uncontrollable temper.

There is, of course, another kind of anger—righteous anger, or anger in the face of injustice or wrong. This is the anger that moved Jesus to take a whip and drive the money changers from the temple. "Take these things out of here!" he said. "Stop making my Father's house a marketplace!" (John 2:16).

Righteous anger is the fuel that causes our moral sense to burn hot in the face of injustice. It is a legacy from our Lord and from the prophets, and every spiritually mature person knows what it is.

What do we admire when we esteem the virtue of self-control in others? Not the absence of anger, for then self-control would be no virtue. The repression of anger is moral suicide. For when we deny our anger, we kill the moral instinct with which it is invariably linked.

Every human virtue rests on the foundation of the self's moral impulse to preserve and guard the dignity of life. When Jesus taught that we should love our neighbor as ourselves (Matt. 22:39), he witnessed to this truth, for he assumed that the virtue of love rests upon the moral foundation of respect for one's own life.

Self-control begins with assuming responsibility for the moral value of one's own life and extends to concern for the lives of others. We lose control over anger when we confuse anger with the moral instinct that propels it. As we shall see, by itself the emotion of anger is blind and without discrimination. Unchecked, it can and will rage out of control. The *feelings* that lead to anger, on the other hand, are sensitive to moral instruction and direction. When we see how those feelings that produce anger can be redirected toward intentions that better serve the good of self and others, we will have identified the virtue of self-control.

Why does anger cause us to lose self-control? Why is it so easy to give way to anger and become blind and insensitive to the damage and destruction that can follow? An analysis of a biblical story about anger may help us answer these questions.

Why Are You Angry?

The subject of anger is introduced in the Bible's earliest account of human violence. Cain and Abel, the sons of Adam and Eve, each prepare offerings to bring to God. One assumes that their parents had instructed them in the purpose for this, as well as in the manner in which it was to be done.

Cain, a tiller of the ground by profession, brought an offering of grain that he had prepared, perhaps in the form of bread prepared from ground grain. Abel, a keeper of sheep, brought a portion of a lamb he had slain. The Bible tells us that the Lord had regard for Abel and his offering, but for Cain and his offering he had no regard. "So Cain was very angry, and his countenance fell. The LORD said to Cain, 'Why are you angry, and why has your countenance fallen? If you do well, will you not be accepted? And if you do not do well, sin is lurking at the door; its desire is for you, but you must master it'" (Gen. 4:4–7).

God's rejection of Cain's offering was met with anger, clearly visible in Cain's facial expression and perhaps his body language. What I said earlier about the emotion of anger can account for Cain's response. A feeling precedes anger. In this case, Cain's reaction shows that his feelings have been hurt. Despite the fact that he apparently acted contrary to known rules for sacrifice, Cain took God's rejection of his sacrifice as personal rejection. After all, his occupation was that of raising grain for food, not sheep for slaughter. He was no doubt good at his profession and brought what he felt was the best he had to offer. Rejection of our best will cause a stinging blow to our self-worth.

As if that was not enough, his brother's offering was accepted, and one can imagine the difficulty Abel had in concealing his own pleasure from Cain! Now Cain feels doubly offended, with his brother gaining a privilege and recognition that he himself desperately sought. Am I reading too much into the story to suggest that Cain might feel that his own rights were violated and that his feeling was one of moral outrage as well as personal pique? In light of what took place next, I think not.

Anger gave expression and direction to Cain's feelings. Anger acted out directly toward the Lord may not have been an option for Cain. But his brother Abel is a clear target, for jealous anger must always have an object. Cain's sense of being treated unfairly now surfaces in light of what appears to be Abel's preferential treatment by the Lord.

Cain is angry. The fuse is lit. The crime scene is developing. God seeks to intervene. "Why are you angry? . . . If you do well, you will be accepted. . . . Sin is lurking at the door; its desire is for you, but you must master it."

Cain's anger itself may not yet be a sin against God, nor against his brother. His anger is not yet an uncontrollable passion that renders him helpless. Cain needs to regain self-control, and there is every indication that this is still within his power. What Cain must "master" is not the emotion of anger but the moral direction of his anger. Because anger is fueled by moral passion, it can be disarmed by attention to its moral consequences as they are directed toward others. That which is "lurking at the door" in Cain's life is the unacknowledged and unthinkable act of murdering his brother as the only way of satisfying his twisted sense of moral justice. Mastering the sin that lurks at the door has nothing to do with repressing the emotion of anger but everything to do with taking responsibility for the direction anger takes in seeking its vindication. If Cain cannot master this lurking sin, disaster lies ahead.

Unfortunately, Cain was not touched by the therapeutic probing of the divine counselor. Enter violence! Cain's passion to defend his own rights now fuels the rage of jealousy. Cain's anger provides all the emotional energy he needs to commit violence in an attempt to even the score, to deliver a verdict, to punish the one who has robbed him of what he cherished most—his pride. Cain kills Abel, whose blood spills on the ground.

When the Lord confronts Cain with the question, "Where is your brother?" Cain cynically attempts to deflect the question by asking another: "Am I my brother's keeper?" The implied but unspoken response is: "No, you are not your brother's keeper, you are your brother's brother!"

Let's look at anger from a more contemporary perspective. The blood of Cain as well as that of Abel runs in our veins.

"She Made Me So Angry!"

Jim's comment at the beginning of this chapter ("Maybe I'm addicted to anger!") was not meant to be taken seriously. But he may have been closer to the truth than he realized. Anger can be addictive when it produces the stimulation and adrenaline "rush" we need to compensate for the empty feeling of being powerless and worthless. The frequency of his outbursts of temper and the increasing level of violence that accompanied these rages bothered Jim.

The most recent episode, which prompted his seeking counsel, had occurred during a quarrel with his wife over his failure to renew the registration for the car, resulting in a traffic citation for her, a fine, and a penalty. As Jim remembered the incident, it was when she reminded him that he had been late in paying some other bills that he blew up. "I said a lot of hurtful things, I am sure," Jim recalled. "But she made me so angry! Then I really lost it and grabbed a favorite vase of hers and threw it against the wall. She told me that I had better get control of myself before I began to hit her. How do you control yourself when you are so angry you can't think straight?"

"She made me so angry!" Most of us in recounting an incident in which someone has wronged us will say, "He made me so angry," or, "Just thinking about it makes me angry." It is almost instinctive for parents to say to their children when they are acting up, "You make me so angry!"

Well, what's wrong with that? Don't other people sometimes "make us angry"? No! I stir up anger in my own emotional laboratory, having all of the right ingredients close at hand. What other people do is stimulate *feelings* in us. Jim's wife is angry because she felt humiliated and helpless when she was apprehended with an expired car registration. Her experience produced these feelings, which she then turned into anger against Jim as she thought of his failure to take care of these matters.

Confronted by his failure, Jim had *feelings* of shame and perhaps guilt because he had allowed the registration to expire. Such feelings are not pleasant and can lead to a sense of unworthiness and self-blame. In order to deal with these negative feelings about himself, he attempts to deflect them onto someone or something else. When his wife confronted him with his failure, it became a case of attacking the messenger who brought the bad news! In the lens of his experience, she has added insult to injury, reminding him of his pattern of failures, violating his personhood, robbing him of the last vestiges of his dignity.

So Jim attributes his anger to her—"she made me so angry"—as though this could account for his losing control and even for his violence. Whatever shame Jim may have felt for his outburst, he still cannot accept responsibility for his own anger for two reasons. First, he has acquired an internal defense mechanism that deflects his uncontrollable temper to incidents, objects, and persons. Logically, he cannot be held responsible for things outside his control. So when he goes out of control, he blames his uncontrollable anger on external objects and persons. Second, he has allowed his moral instinct for self-preservation to become confused with his anger. It is because Jim perceives that his wife's words have unjustly robbed him of his worth and dignity that he feels justified in blaming his anger on her actions, thereby refusing to take responsibility for it himself.

Until we understand the often hidden connection between moral passions and our emotions we will fail to find the point of intervention into what usually appears to be uncontrollable anger.

Jim now asks, "How do you control yourself when you are so angry you can't think straight?" Jim knows that self-control is a virtue. He admires it in others and deplores the lack in his own life. The shame and guilt that follow his outbursts only drive him deeper into remorse and self-pity, both of which are the offspring of wounded pride. One cannot help the children without healing the parent.

Self-control is rooted in the moral sense of self-worth. The worth of the human self is a divine endowment that carries the remembrance of divine blessing and affirmation (Gen. 1:28, 31). Because we inherited moral shame through our first parents (an internal as well as historical fact), we are born with a tendency toward moral outrage when we feel that defect exposed. Tragically, moral outrage does not result in enhanced moral worth but in its precise opposite. This is why anger is so morally delicious and satisfying when we give way to it, but so self-defeating and shaming when it is viewed in retrospect.

We admire people who can express their anger without losing control more than we do people who "never become angry." This is because self-control is a virtue, not a personality trait. "Be angry but do not sin," the apostle counseled (Eph. 4:26). Paul himself knew something about anger! Perhaps this is why we should listen to him.

In Paul's heated confrontation with his friend and former partner, Barnabas, Luke tells us that "the disagreement became so sharp that they parted company" (Acts 15:39). The Greek word used is *paroxusmos*, which we use today in speaking of someone who has lost their temper so completely that they are uncontrollable. Years later, in writing to the Corinthian church, Paul wrote of the virtue of love and said love "does not insist on its own way; it is not irritable" (1 Cor. 13:5). The word translated as "irritable" is a form of the same Greek word *paroxusmos*. Paul says that love does not have paroxysms because it does not give way to its own impulses and drives.

The Virtue of Self-Control

Let me suggest some specific ways to achieve the virtue of self-control.

1. *Cultivate the moral garden of the inner self.* The metaphor of a garden suggests both planting and weeding. There are "moral seeds" that can grow into weeds. A weed is simply a plant that does not produce the fruit one intends but diverts the nutrients intended for other plants to its own use.

I have suggested that behind the emotion of anger there is a primitive moral instinct that seeks to defend the self against violation and that seeks the recovery of a perceived loss. A garden is produced by intentional care. Benign neglect is as likely to produce bad results as malicious vandalism.

How do we cultivate our moral garden? By tracing out the moral intention of our feelings as though they were to become mature actions. A young man constantly complained about his mother, who happened to live in another city. He expressed anger toward her for wrongs he perceived she had done to him when he lived at home. His anger was like a cancer eating away at his inner life. It would subside for a time but arise whenever he needed someone to blame for the failures and frustrations in his life. I finally suggested to him that we plan her funeral. He was shocked and said that she was not dead and had no signs of ill health. "But," I said quietly, "you have such anger toward her that you surely are planning to kill her, are you not? After all, she has robbed you of all joy and pleasure and has taken away your value as a person."

He was scandalized at my suggestion but finally said, "I see your point. I really don't intend to do her any harm. So I am slowly destroying my own life with anger at her." It is not that simple, of course. But every feeling that is allowed to grow into an emotion can be expressed in the form of an intention. The moral significance of feelings is in what they become as intentions. When we refuse to accept the logical intentions of our feelings because they would be morally unacceptable if carried out, we are weeding our moral garden.

In one of his poignant poems, Lord Byron put it this way:

Meantime I seek no sympathies nor need;
The thorns which I have reap'd are of the tree
I planted,—they have torn me,—and I bleed:
I should have known what fruit would spring from such a
    seed.[1]

Indeed. We achieve self-control when we assume moral responsibility for our feelings as though they were intentions. When God prompted Cain to reflect upon his anger, he was asking him to "master" the sin that was lurking at the door in the form of a hidden intention of violence toward his brother. We tease out the moral content of our anger when we answer the question: "What do I intend to do with this anger?"

If we wish to achieve the virtue of self-control, we must begin by taking inventory of our emotions with regard to the specific intentions hidden in each. The habitual use of anger to justify and satisfy our inner sense of moral outrage will cause us to resist this exercise. The result of taking such a serious moral inventory of our feelings is this: As we reject the inappropriate—indeed, the immoral—tendencies of our feelings, we will achieve the moral virtue of self-control.

2. *Communicate how we feel when our feelings are hurt.* What if Cain had said to the Lord: "I am not sure why my offering was rejected, but I want you to know that I feel rejected and shamed, as though I have lost favor in your sight"? Instead, Cain projected his feelings through anger and found a target in his brother Abel. What blocked the Lord's therapeutic touch with Cain was the unwillingness of Cain to locate and express the feelings behind his anger. The question "Why are you angry?" was the right question. Cain was unwilling to find the answer.

We achieve the virtue of self-control by taking a moral inventory of our feelings as if they were intentions. But this will not be possible if we are unable or unwilling to discover the feelings that lie behind the emotion of anger. Anger happens so quickly that we often miss the feeling stage prior to the emotion. We need to ask "Why am I angry?" relentlessly until we discover the core feelings that produced the anger.

We can only break the habit of saying "You made me so angry" by asking, "Why am I really angry?" Our first response will usually be to cite some action or words that caused us to be angry. Or, to point to some circumstance beyond our control that made us angry. We then need to ask the further question, "What did I feel that made me so angry?" If we ask this relentlessly until we discover the core feelings, we will then be able to activate the moral inventory and cultivate our moral garden.

3. *Create a space for grace in our life.* Self-control is a "grace-full" life. We admire the virtue of self-control in others because we see it as a way of living gracefully. Grace needs space. The problem with bitterness, envy, strife, jealousy, and anger, to name a few of the siblings produced by the parents of wounded pride, is that these not only take emotional energy to maintain, they take up space on the "hard drive" of our operating system, to borrow computer terminology.

Earlier in this chapter I made the passing comment that our entrance into this world is not pretty and is usually painful, if not downright indecent. "Someone needs to be forgiven for that," I commented. A feeling that is charged with the moral passion of righting a wrong and recovering a sense of self-worth cannot be ignored or dismissed. A feeling cannot be healed by moral argument but only by another moral feeling.

If I feel that I have been wronged and become angry, it is of no help to be told that I ought not to feel that way and that my anger is inappropriate. Moral persuasion does not heal what is perceived as moral injustice. This is why grace is needed. Grace operates by giving over one's moral hurt to a higher moral power. Love is the highest moral power, greater than law or any judicial system. The pain created by a perceived moral wrong seeks more than justice; it seeks the healing power of love. This is the spiritual dimension of healing and recovery of self-control.

2

Self-Confidence

Being Assertive without Being Aggressive

I myself, Paul, appeal to you by the meekness and gentleness of Christ—I who am humble when face to face with you, but bold toward you when I am away!

2 Corinthians 10:1

There is a line in the 1960s musical, *Hair,* sung by one of the lead characters named Claude. "I believe in God and God believes in Claude!" Besides the fact that it has a nice poetic ring to it, the expression conveys the essence of self-confidence. One does not have to have a name that rhymes with God to venture the same conviction. Being confident of God's belief in me is the other half of my belief in God! And, as I cannot speak for him, I hear and believe what he says of me before I speak for myself.

This is quite different from the conventional wisdom farmers shared with their neighbors in the coffee shop in the town where I grew up in rural middle America: "God helps those who help themselves." As a moral judgment against sloth, the axiom hit its target with deadly accuracy. As a maxim by which to achieve self-confidence, it renders God virtually unnecessary as long as the self is capable of maintaining its own health, success, and good fortune. Ironically, when suffering catastrophic losses to livestock and crops from disease and weather, those same farmers quickly blamed the Almighty and excused themselves. They never had "farming failures"; it was always a "crop failure"!

What Self-Confidence Is Not

How do we define self-confidence? Let me say what I believe it is not. Self-confidence is *not* the sticky sweetness that oozes from an inner sanctuary of spiritual smugness. Nor is it the "in your face" moral certitude of those with a ravenous appetite for feasting on moral lapses in others. There is nothing that attracts us to such persons. Indeed, we become uncomfortable in their presence and suspicious of their motives. None of us wants to be a convenient wall on which the self-assured can write their slogans, nor be competitors in a game where it is always "full court press."

Self-confidence is *not* pretty when it is the result of self-deception, as was the case in *The Emperor's New Clothes.* The emperor was a fool for parading his self-confidence without reality testing!

Spiritual smugness can be as aggressive as moral certitude. Please, if these be self-confidence, let me be the companion of those who have a healthy measure of self-doubt!

What Self-Confidence Is

One way of defining self-confidence is to ask, What is it that we admire in others when they tackle a task too hard or too difficult for them, as though they knew something hidden from us? What is it that enables some people to assert their own dignity and worth in the face of slanderous attack and abusive behavior, as though they possess some inner truth they will not allow to be trampled? We all know such people and applaud the virtue of self-confidence when we see it worn appropriately and without pretense.

Jesus is one example.

At his baptism, Jesus heard the voice of God from heaven: "You are my Son, the Beloved; with you I am well pleased" (Luke 3:22). Later, when he was accused of harboring a demon, Jesus simply responded, "You dishonor me. Yet I do not seek my own glory; there is one who seeks it and he is the judge" (John 8:49–50). We admire him for his composure in the face of such an attack on his person. The truth he would not allow anyone to violate was the truth of his own being. The echo of his baptism, "You are my Son, the Beloved," answered back the malicious accusations of his accusers. The basis for his self-confidence was his confidence in who he was as God's beloved Son.

When his own disciples lost sight of the goal and tried to dissuade him from taking that last trip to Jerusalem, he rebuked them and said, "If any want to become my followers, let them deny themselves and take up their cross and follow me. For those who want to save their life will lose it, and those who lose their life for my sake will find it. For what will it profit them if they gain the whole world but forfeit their life? Or what will they give in return for their life?" (Matt. 16:24–26). Confident that his life was moving toward fulfillment rather than loss, he was able to proceed with self-confidence when those around him drew back in fear and uncertainty. We admire him for his steadfastness in the face of confusion in those who were closest to him.

When tormented and troubled by the knowledge of his own impending death on the cross, Jesus acknowledged his own ambivalence and said: "Now my soul is troubled. And what should I say—'Father, save me from this hour'? No, it is for this reason that I have come to this hour" (John 12:27). Confident that "his hour had come" (John 13:1), Jesus seized the moment with utter self-confidence that even this death was "his death" and could be accepted as congruent with the purpose for which he was sent as the "beloved Son." We admire him for the inner assurance that brought into focus the whole of his life in the moment when reason flees and emotion fails.

Composure, steadfastness, and inner assurance—these are some aspects of what we mean by self-confidence. We admire persons who exhibit these qualities in the face of adversity, attack, and anxious fear. Self-confidence refuses to regret the life one has lived, and turns chaotic confusion into a defining moment of one's very being.

But this was Jesus, you say, and he had the advantage of being without sin as well as being the divine Son of God. Well, that is true. But the self-confidence of Jesus was not a divine virtue—I don't know that we think of one of the qualities of God as self-confidence!—but self-confidence is a human virtue precisely because it rises up out of the depths of the human spirit under all kinds of adversity. "Being found in human form," writes the apostle Paul, Jesus "humbled himself and became obedient to the point of death" (Phil. 2:8). The author of the Book of Hebrews tells us that, as our high priest, Jesus is able to sympathize with our weakness because "in every respect" he was tempted as we are (Heb. 4:15).

Jesus' sinlessness was possible only because he was the divine Son of God; but his virtue of self-confidence was possible because Jesus the man went willingly and obediently to the death he had accepted in becoming human. The utter confidence of this sinless Jesus in his own life and mission—his obedient acceptance of his God-ordained death—becomes all the more remarkable when we consider that death itself is the result of sin. "For our sake [God] made him to be sin who knew no sin" (2 Cor. 5:21).

There was no spiritual smugness in Jesus, nor did he prey upon others in order to demonstrate his own moral certitude. The religious leaders of his day demonstrated both qualities and were not admired by the common people. In contrast, all of those who were viewed as unworthy by the same leaders were drawn to Jesus precisely because he asserted the truth of his own life and mission as the sign of God's gracious kingdom of healing and hope.

Let me give another example—this time of one who was radically transformed from his false moral certitude and religious smugness into an apostle of love. Saul of Tarsus was rightly feared by the early Christians for his fanatical zeal and murderous mission of hunting down believers in Jesus. Luke says that when he was "still breathing threats and murder against the disciples," he encountered the risen Christ on the road to Damascus and was dramatically converted (Acts 9:1). Later, having taken the name Paul, he spoke of his former life as being confident "in the flesh," and blameless before the law. All of this, Paul wrote, he came to regard as loss because of Christ. All his former moral and religious certainty he called "rubbish" and spoke only of the confidence that he had gained in becoming a follower of Christ. "Brothers and sisters, join in imitating me," he urged his readers (Phil. 3:4, 8, 17). This is self-confidence of the most attractive kind!

Do we find the virtues of composure, steadfastness, and inner assurance in Paul as well? Absolutely. Self-confidence of this kind did not come easy for him. By his own admission he had not achieved it but said, "I press on to make it my own" (Phil. 3:12). We only need mention the quarrel he had with Barnabas over John Mark, whom he felt had failed in quitting their first missionary journey. Paul was so certain of his own judgment in the matter that he parted from Barnabas and took on Silas as his partner

(Acts 15:36–41). This incident was surely one that Paul did not like to remember.

Later in Paul's life we see a different kind of self-confidence. After completing his third missionary journey, he announced his plan to return to Jerusalem with the offering that had been collected from the churches for relief of the Christians in Judea who were suffering famine. This is how he explained it to the elders from the church at Ephesus: "And now, as a captive to the Spirit, I am on my way to Jerusalem, not knowing what will happen to me there, except that the Holy Spirit testifies to me in every city that imprisonment and persecutions are waiting for me. But I do not count my life of any value to myself, if only I may finish my course and the ministry that I received from the Lord Jesus, to testify to the good news of God's grace" (Acts 20:22–24).

So far so good. What happened next, however, becomes a case study in self-confidence. When Paul and his company set sail for Jerusalem, they arrived at the port of Tyre in Syria. Looking up the believers in the local church at Tyre, Paul and company stayed with them seven days. As Luke reports it, "Through the Spirit they told Paul not to go on to Jerusalem" (Acts 21:4). There is no mention made of any change in Paul's plans, and the next day they set out for Jerusalem, despite this prophetic message, apparently given by the Spirit of God!

Arriving in Caesarea, they lodged at the house of Philip the evangelist. At this time, a prophet by the name of Agabus came from Judea and, binding his own feet and hands with Paul's belt, said, "Thus says the Holy Spirit, 'This is the way the Jews in Jerusalem will bind the man who owns this belt and will hand him over to the Gentiles.'" When they heard this, Luke reported, they "urged him not to go up to Jerusalem." Paul's response was: "What are you doing, weeping and breaking my heart? For I am ready not only to be bound but even to die in Jerusalem for the name of the Lord Jesus." Luke adds, "Since he would not be persuaded, we remained silent except to say, 'The Lord's will be done'" (Acts 21:11–14).

Paul's composure in the face of the direct attack on his plan by those who claimed to speak in the name of the Holy Spirit is remarkable. So certain were those who sought to dissuade him of the folly of this trip that they invoked the very authority of the Spirit of God on their side! Steadfastly, Paul maintained his direction despite the rather constant attempts by those closest to him to turn him back. As for inner assurance concerning his mission, Paul never wavered. He thought of his life as "captive to the Spirit" and acknowledged that he had no assurance that he would successfully evade the dire consequences others warned would befall his trip to Jerusalem.

As it turned out, they were right. Paul was quickly arrested, barely escaped death at the hands of the Jewish leaders who were fanatically committed to his death, and ended up spending two years in prison and finally arrived in chains as a prisoner in Rome. Writing to the church at Philippi from his prison cell at Rome, Paul appears to have no regrets. "I want you to know, beloved that what has happened to me has actually helped to spread the gospel, so that it has become known throughout the whole imperial guard and to everyone else that my imprisonment is for Christ; and most of the brothers and sisters, having been made confident in the Lord by my imprisonment, dare to speak the word with greater boldness and without fear" (Phil. 1:12–14).

Not to Regret One's Life

Self-confidence, I have said, refuses to regret the life one has lived. Even more, it turns chaotic confusion into a defining moment of one's very being. Perhaps this is the clue to the secret of self-confidence. The opposite of self-confidence is not self-doubt but self-regret. The absence

of self-doubt, as we have seen, can lead to spiritual smugness and a false moral certitude, both of which can aggressively attack and destroy a relationship. Self-confidence
always struggles with and overcomes self-doubt. It does
not try to deny it as a means of gaining absolute certitude. For when one acts with absolute certainty only to
discover that it was the wrong action, regret invariably
follows.

Jesus began his ministry in a glorious manifestation of
power over disease, demons, and death that afflicted others. Taking no credit for himself, he attributed this power
to the Spirit of God working through him. Rather than
building up his self-confidence as the Messiah through the
miraculous deeds he was able to accomplish, Jesus found
composure, steadfastness, and inner assurance as he rested
on the knowledge of who he was. Did he regret not accepting the opportunity to turn stone into bread and achieving
fame and recognition as a miracle worker? Certainly not!
Did he regret not seeking more aggressively to impose the
Kingdom of God upon unwilling subjects? Hardly! In
asserting the truth of his own life and mission, he resisted
the temptation to aggressive self-promotion that would
violate the integrity of those to whom he came with good
news.

Not to regret one's life. Not to reject one's life as worthless as a means to gain some final spiritual virtue is the
mark of self-confidence. Even Paul, whom we have used
as a case study in self-confidence, though he acknowledged the worthlessness of his religious pretension prior
to becoming a Christian, did not reject or regret his life
but found reason to believe, retroactively, that his entire
life, from conception onward, was destined to be of service to God. Paul's confidence is that "God, who had set
me apart before I was born and called me through his
grace"(Gal. 1:15) is the one who underscored his entire
life. Paul did not regret his life for a moment, though he

acknowledged the wrongdoing for which he received God's mercy and grace.

Being Assertive without Being Aggressive

Judy (not her real name) is a married woman who is active in her church and views her role of wife and mother as a deeply spiritual task. She attempts to model for her children and her husband what she considers to be Christ-like attitudes and behavior. She is submissive to her husband's demands, sensitive to her children's needs, lenient in administering punishment, and, like a sponge, she soaks up the emotional pain of everyone.

"I know that I should not complain," she reported one day in my office. "But sometimes I feel like a doormat for everyone to walk over and an emotional punching bag for everyone to unload their negative feelings on." As a woman might do who self-consciously checks to see that her hair is in place after being caught in a sudden draft, she applied a bit of spiritual cosmetic by adding: "I do find the Lord a great help to me, and I do not know what I would do without him."

There was a long pause.

"What is it that hurts the most?" I asked.

The dam burst and her pain flowed in torrents, carrying her along like an unmanned river raft. She recounted humiliating and emotionally abusive incidents in which her husband had berated her for real and imagined failures in her discipline of the children, her domestic chores, and her inadequacy as a sexual partner.

The river runs wild.

Struggling to stay afloat on the raging current of feelings pent up too long, a litany of minor incidents overflowed into a lagoon of self-pity and wretched self-recrimination.

"I'm a miserable person," she whimpered. "I hate myself for being so weak. My friends tell me that I should be more aggressive and stand up for myself. I've tried that. And my children tell me that they hate me. My husband asks, 'Where did all of your religion go?' I don't know how Jesus did it, but I am no Jesus. I guess I'm not much of anything."

I report this not to suggest appropriate therapeutic strategies in counseling but to cut an opening into the windowless cell where the self cowers, lacking self-confidence. Caught in the double bind of a spirituality that forbids self-assertion while, at the same time, demanding self-giving, Judy is an example of a person who lacks spiritual fitness.

She lacks the inner assurance of her own value as a person and the confidence to assert herself in the face of humiliating attacks and unreasonable demands. The script that she replays in her own mind is one of self-indictment and shame. She is a victim of emotional self-abuse, cloaked in the guise of spirituality. She has neither heard nor assimilated the good news that she is a "beloved child" of God, so she has no confidence in making that assertion on her own behalf. A theology that annihilates our self-confidence and causes us to regret our life is a false theology, contrary to God's desire and purpose.

Without the self-confidence that comes from the inner assurance of her own worth as defined and upheld by the grace of God, a person lacks the composure and steadfastness to assert the meaning and purpose of her own life. Like Job, she may even come to regret the fact of her own existence. In desperation, she may even turn to violence against others or herself.

The woman in South Carolina who sent the car with her two children into a lake to drown is one example. The woman in Long Beach, California, who threw her two children off the bridge into the Los Angeles River and then jumped in herself is another. Still other examples are embittered employees who storm into their workplace to gun down and kill all whom they imagine to be responsible for their own misery. These people turn their inner self-hatred into murderous aggression.

Lack of self-confidence is not a sign of humility nor is it a spiritual virtue. It is a wound in the self that will not stop bleeding. God's salvation comes in the form of divine surgery where the wound is closed, the bleeding stanched, and the spirit of the self renewed so that life again begins to flow like "a stream of water [guided] by the hand of the Lord" (Prov. 21:1).

Restoration of self-confidence requires more than emotional repair. It begins with spiritual renewal. True spirituality is not a religious mask to cover a deficit of self-confidence. We are spiritual beings at the very core, and self-confidence involves asserting the value of the self, the renewal that results from a full acceptance of the unique human spirit that we are. King David, who used aggression to take a woman who belonged to another and then had her husband killed to conceal the deed, sought and found this spiritual renewal.

"You desire truth in the inward being," he said to God, "therefore teach me wisdom in my secret heart. . . . Create in me a clean heart, O God, and put a new and right spirit within me. . . . Restore to me the joy of your salvation, and sustain in me a willing spirit. . . . O Lord, open my lips, and my mouth will declare your praise" (Ps. 51:6, 10, 12, 15).

We admire those who exhibit the virtue of self-confidence. But as so often happens, the virtues we admire in others make our own deficits more obvious. This is particularly true with self-confidence. For self-confidence begins with acceptance of the self as a gift to cherish and a spirit to grow.

Here, then, are three steps to help us achieve self-confidence—to help us gain the composure, steadfastness, and inner assurance that brings into focus our whole life.

1. Acknowledge, as King David did, that we have a broken spirit that needs renewal. "The sacrifice acceptable to God is a broken spirit; a broken and contrite heart, O God, you will not despise" (Ps. 51:17). A broken spirit is not a

bad spirit, it is just a *broken* spirit that needs healing. The fact that God does not despise a broken spirit is good news! We despise our own broken spirits, but God does not. When I am confident that my spirit is broken and that God, like a loving parent, can fix it, I have achieved the beginning of self-confidence. I can now offer my broken spirit to him for renewal.

2. Open our lips, as David suggested in his psalm, and begin to declare the good news that our spirit has been restored and that we have recovered the boundary of our self. This truth we must guard with vigilance, not agreeing with those who seek to violate or shame us. No one else can effectively assert our own worth and dignity as a child of God. Once Jesus heard the voice from heaven say, "You are my Son, the beloved; with you I am well pleased," it was left to Jesus to assert this for himself!

3. Make out of the crises and struggles of life a "defining moment" in which we assert the truth of who we are— even as we accept what cannot be changed, reject what cannot be true, and find composure in caring for what cannot be lost when the river rises and the foundations move.

We will know that we have self-confidence when we move beyond admiring the self-confidence of others and value our own response in those moments when life puts us to the test.

3

Courage

Overcoming Fear
without Being Foolhardy

> Though we had already suffered and been shamefully mistreated at Philippi, as you know, we had courage in our God to declare to you the gospel of God in spite of great opposition.
>
> 1 Thessalonians 2:2

We admire persons who demonstrate courage because we all know the feeling of fear. We know that courage is not the absence of fear but doing what is necessary and of great value despite being afraid. The person who rushes into a burning building to rescue a child demonstrates courage not because that is what we expect of everyone but because her action is extraordinary in light of the danger to her own life. Some have lost their own lives in such attempts, and we still honor them for their courage.

Where does courage come from? Children are not born with it, because they have not yet learned fear. While there may be a prenatal instinct similar to what we call fear, I am speaking of fear as an emotion that results from experience and knowledge. When the infant begins to distinguish between the familiar face of the caretaker and the unknown face of a stranger, the emotion of fear begins to develop. When children become aware of danger, fear can become a paralyzing restriction.

After a few painful failures at attempting to walk, the infant who once crawled trustingly off the edge of the bed with no knowledge or fear of height has to be coaxed to let go of the chair in order to take the first successful steps alone. The fearful distance between the outstretched hand of the parent and the reach of the child is overcome by the expectation of a safe arrival and a warm hug. Courage is developed as fear is overcome by the anticipation of successful accomplishment.

Why Courage Is a Virtue

The virtue of courage is tied to the value of an act to the self. If an act provides no value to the self it does not require courage. Picture the child who ventures the first step without the security of holding on to an object. He is finding the greater value of reaching the outstretched arms of the parent over the security of holding fast to an anchor point. The child wants the parent to come closer so that the gap is closed. Fear seeks to bring love to its side. But the parent resists this entreaty and refuses to move. Instead, the parent coaxes the child all the more to cross what the parent knows is a safe distance but for the child is experienced as an unknown, even fearful chasm. Finally the child ventures the precarious few steps and collapses into the waiting arms. Love demands that fear be overcome in order to reach the goal love offers. Only then is courage born and fear "cast out."

This may be what John meant when he wrote, "There is no fear in love, but perfect love casts out fear" (1 John 4:18). We cannot cast out our own fear by using our own love. That is not how it works. No, it is the love of others, as they encourage us, that "casts out fear" by enabling us to summon up the courage required to move toward what love offers as of supreme value to the self.

The value that fuels courage, then, is the admiration and appreciation that others extend to us and that becomes internalized as self-worth and self-esteem. Courage, therefore, is a virtue because it requires that we respond to the love of others in pursuit of acts that are of value to the self.

Where an action produces only dramatic stimulation and not admiration based on its moral qualities, it is not courage but foolhardiness. We do not think of one who gambles, for example, as a person who has courage simply because he wagers the rent money against formidable odds at Las Vegas. We do not admire those who are foolhardy, and if we do, we reveal our own addiction to risk-taking.

When taking risks becomes an addiction, we see clearly the distinction between courage and compulsive risk-taking. For one addicted to gambling, the degree of risk involved increases as the need for stimulation grows. Because the "narcotic" effect is produced by the taking of a risk rather than the "payoff," beating the odds produces no lasting or intrinsic satisfaction. The occasional payoff seems to offer a rationale for the taking of risks, but it is always reinvested and usually lost in subsequent gambling. For the compulsive gambler no fortune is final. Fear is the masked enemy behind compulsion that chooses its own battlefield and sets its own terms. We may be allowed to choose our own weapons in seeking to overcome fear, but the game is the same and the odds are always against us.

It is not courage that drives the compulsive risk-taker to attempt dangerous and death-defying feats, nor is courage generated by such attempts. The daredevil stunts of Evil Knievel, for example, thrilled the crowd precisely because there was great danger involved. Is it his courage that attracts spectators to these events, or the voyeuristic thrill of watching somebody get hurt or possibly killed? Do those who cheer the matador in the bullring attend for the purpose of cheering his courage, or to play out their own fears in a vicarious but safe role reversal? I do not know. I have never been a spectator at such events, and the only bulls I have feared are the ones from which I fled on the family farm. But in the bullring, if there was never a chance of being gored by the bull, I suspect that the spectacle would be boring rather than thrilling.

One thing I know. I do not draw courage from watching someone push the envelope of his or her own fear to the edge. I suspect that those who gamble with the real values of life—and even their own lives—for the sake of the thrill never overcome their fear and thus do not really develop more courage. We hear occasionally of someone playing Russian Roulette with a pistol, where only one bullet is loaded with the other chambers left empty, who ends up firing the fatal shot into his head. We never hear of those who play the game for the sake of developing more courage so as to face the real challenges of life. No one seriously offers this tragic game as a way to achieve courage.

There is something fatalistic about fear. What we fear most of all is fear itself. And it is fear that drives us to compulsive acts. Fear will not leave us alone until it maims us or kills us.

When Fear Casts Out Love

We are at a loss to explain why some refuse to engage in "safe sex" when they are sexually promiscuous. Indeed, we are at a loss to account for the compulsive risk-taking by those who seek intimacy through a series of sexual partners, especially for women who are vulnerable to abuse, degradation, and sometimes violent death. No one views such behavior as courageous, though the dangers are real and the potential loss horrendous. Those who take such risks may be attempting to bring love to the side of fear. Instead of love "casting out fear," however, it is fear that casts out love. In trying to find love by "feasting on fear," the venue changes but the menu remains the same. The appetite of fear devours love under the guise of fearlessness.

For people who live like this, every encounter must be a conquest and every lover a victim. Each time shame is felt over the price one must pay to bring love to the side of fear, the mask of fearlessness is quickly assumed. Each time love attempts to cast out hidden fear and heal its shame, love is cast out. Fear remains. These people are brave and beautiful, in their own eyes. They are pictures of sadness and sorrow for those who love and lament.

When we think of those who live such futile lives, the words of Jude haunt us: "These are blemishes on your love-feasts, while they feast with you without fear, feeding themselves. They are waterless clouds carried along by the winds; autumn trees without fruit, twice dead, uprooted" (Jude 12). Feasting without fear, feeding themselves—this is not courage, but cannibalism. The appetite of fear is never satisfied but requires new offerings of the self as a sacrifice upon its altar of terror.

So fearlessness is not the absence of fear, but a defense against it. Fearlessness is fear's full dress uniform seeking a parade and a prize. By putting on fearlessness, one seeks to overcome fear by feeding it with the illusion of power and invulnerability.

Courage is more humble and far more realistic. It accepts fear as a necessary part of life. Without courage, fear would never permit us to open the door to life and love. It takes courage to hope and to have faith when we know fear. It takes courage to live with our weaknesses, our vulnerability, our loneliness. It takes courage to live with fear.

The Courage to Live with Fear

Foolhardiness makes the mistake of attempting to overcome or deny normal and healthy fear. Normal fear is the fear that one should feel when an internal alarm goes off warning us that we are venturing beyond what is good or safe for us. Normal fear is the emotion that one should feel when threatened by an object, force, or person that has the potential of injuring or violating our own space and personal being.

Healthy fear is fear grounded in the instinct for self-preservation at the physical level, self-care at the personal level, and self-worth at the spiritual level.

Because we are created in the image of God, we ought to fear God, which means to have reverence and respect for his power and holiness (Gen. 20:11; Prov. 1:7; Rom. 3:18). Not to fear God is a spiritual deficit, a deficiency of self-worth as the objects of God's love and care.

We ought to fear that which would demean or violate our integrity as persons of value created in God's image. We ought to fear that which would threaten or destroy our physical life. The instinct for self-preservation, self-care, and self-worth are aspects of the physical, personal, and spiritual life that belong to each person as created in the divine image.

Normal fear is the guardian of the good. It is an ally of the self in a world filled with misadventure and misdemeanor. Normal fear is like a sleeping watchdog, never disturbing our peace but instantly alert to our own missteps and the intrusion of others who might do us harm.

Courage is comfortable with normal fear and has no need to deny or conceal it. At the same time, courage has a vision greater than fear and can override fear when necessary in order to act so as to apprehend or sustain the value it perceives. A mother teaches her child to fear the car that races down the street as a danger to life and limb. The mother's fear is normal, for herself as well as for her child. If the child should dart into the street, however, unaware of the approaching car, the mother will overcome her fear and rush to the aid of the child even though putting her own life in danger.

One could explain her actions as motivated by love, and this would not be wrong. But love can also be traumatized by fear and unable to respond when the object of love is threatened. It is courage, not only love, that overrides the fear and risks danger for the sake of another's life.

We all know that perfect strangers have been known also to risk their own lives under similar circumstances by rushing to the aid of a child caught in the flow of traffic. Courage is not dependent upon the bond of love between it and the object of its action. But love without courage is a cloak of warm sentimentality wrapped around the frozen nerves of fear.

The watchdog of normal fear must be responsive to the commands of courage. One does not have to kill the dog in order to cross the road. Once fear has raised the alarm, its job is done. It is when we allow fear to become master that we either cower behind the wall of self-preservation or send fear to the dark dungeon of our subconscious so we can plunge ahead without fear at our side.

Courage walks with fear at its heels, under control and constantly on the alert. Courage, I have said, has a vision that goes beyond fear. Fear senses danger, while courage sees the value on the other side of danger. Where the value for the self outweighs the threat to the self in a situation fraught with risk and danger, courage emerges as an extraordinary act of self-surrender to the good. The virtue of courage is the value that empowers it. When we find and follow the values that we cherish, we will find the courage to live with our fear.

Being Empowered for Courage

Courage, as the theologian Paul Tillich once said, is the courage to be. In saying this, he pointed to the fact that courage is a state of being before it is a course of action. I have suggested that the virtue of courage is tied to the value the self perceives in taking a particular action. I must add to that now by saying that before an act can have value to me, I must have internalized the value of my own being as affirmed and upheld by the love and care of others.

The value of being loved for who one is becomes the foundational value that empowers courage. This produces the courage for taking first steps.

The child who gains courage to take the first few steps is confronted with an anxious choice between an anchor point that offers security and the unsecured and perilous journey toward an experienced value in the form of a parent with outstretched arms. What produces movement on the part of the child, despite the fear involved, is the known value of the parent that can only be reached by letting go of the anchor point. It would be more difficult for a stranger to induce the child to have the courage to take these steps, for in this case the normal fear would be stronger than the value of reaching the other person.

Even if the child fails in the first few attempts, she is rewarded by hugs and kisses by the parent. The attempt itself is valued as much as success. When the child is valued for her own sake, this becomes an internal value deeper than normal fear. This is the value of personal being that empowers courage in the face of fear. The "courage to be" launches the child into the world where there will be many "first steps," metaphorically speaking. This is the courage that walks with fear at its heels, having it under control.

One way or another, those of us who are physically capable learn to walk. But not all of us have the courage to be. Though we may be physically able, if we lack courage, we are spiritually impaired. For the courage to be is a mark of spiritual fitness, of spiritual balance. We are dependent upon those who first care for us to form the value of self-worth and to empower us with this courage. Ultimately, however, the value of the self is a spiritual reality not a psychological reaction. Courage is a function of the human spirit and not a personality trait.

Spiritual balance issues from our "walk toward God," to extend the metaphor. God arouses within us a spirit of faith, hope, and love by giving us a renewed spirit and then stepping back in order to give us space in which to take our own steps. Is that true? Are we not taught that God is always at our side, that he comes to us whenever we are afraid to comfort us? Yes. But if that is our total concept of God, we have bound God to our fear rather than being ourselves bound to God. Like children who control their parents by manipulation, the spiritually immature call God to the side of their fear. God is then expected to remove anxiety and fear instead of leading us through our fear to grasp the promise held out before us. If we want to have courage—dare I say it!—we must let go of God's hand!

Courage is the spiritual muscle of faith and is only developed where there is sufficient space for us to "walk toward God." The God who comes to us and is present with us is also the God who creates a space that we must cross in order to receive what is promised.

Courage begins with the inner assurance that God loves and values us. Every step we take as we let go of childhood anchor points is with the assurance that God will be there when we fall and will bless us as we finish. Faith in God is the "assurance of things hoped for" (Heb. 11:1), which creates the courage to overcome fear.

The apostle Paul demonstrated this kind of courage when he reminded the Christians in Thessalonica of the circumstances of his first visit. "Though we had already suffered and been shamefully mistreated at Philippi, as you know, we had courage in our God to declare to you the gospel of God in spite of great opposition" (1 Thess. 2:2). Later, Paul remembered this venture as one he took with "fear at his heels." "For even when we came into Macedonia, our bodies had no rest, but we were afflicted in every way—disputes without and fears within" (2 Cor. 7:5). Paul managed these fears, measured the risk, and launched his life into the world with a vision of the "crown" that awaited him at the end (2 Tim. 4:8).

Finding Courage for Everyday Living

Courage is a virtue we admire in others, because it makes visible a quality of the human spirit that we all esteem and desire for ourselves. How can we develop more courage when we feel a lack? Here are some guidelines.

Put a Leash on Your Fears

Fear is meant to walk at your heel, subject to your commands. Name your fears and take each one "out for a walk" as an exercise in gaining control. It may help to seek the aid of a counselor or trusted friend in doing this. You will be surprised to discover how manageable fear is when it is intentionally "put on the leash" and taken with you in the ordinary routines and experiences of life.

Julie, who was driven by a constant fear of death, tried this by going to the cemetery with a friend who had lost her husband to put flowers on the grave, sharing the grief and claiming the promise of life after death. Julie told her friend that she was taking her own fear of death for "a walk" on these excursions. They did this every month or so, and Julie began to manage her fear of death without morbid and compulsive thoughts. She would say that she has found new courage to live with her fear. She has put it on a leash.

Where fears that appear to be compulsive and psychologically driven are identified, seek spiritual and psychological counseling for healing. Remember that courage is not the absence or denial of fear but having it under control so that one can move freely and effectively in achieving personal goals and performing valued tasks.

Get a New Focus for Your Life

The child develops courage by having a clear focal point for each activity. When the focal point is moved too far out of vision, the child loses interest. When the focal point is always within reach, the child becomes bored. The key to courage is having a focal point that is within one's vision but requires extraordinary effort to reach.

My friend Davy, who suffered a motorcycle accident and is now a paraplegic, saw his focal point in life disappear due to his physical disability. He could have resigned himself to total inactivity and become an object of care for others. Instead, he refocused his life and found goals that were attainable, though with great effort and considerable pain. I think of him as a person of great courage, though he dismisses such a suggestion as nonsense. He would say that it doesn't take a lot of courage to move about in a wheelchair—only a lot of patience and time! But I know many who envy the spirit he exhibits as he pursues his own goal in life.

By creating a new focal point that is reasonably attainable, though requiring extraordinary effort, you can, as you once did, take your first steps toward something of value and find courage in doing it.

Open Up Space between You and God

This is not meant to be frivolous! Most people are trying to get close to God, and I am suggesting putting some space between yourself and God! Everything that I have said in this chapter points to the fact that courage is a form of spiritual maturity or fitness. Courage is the spiritual muscle in faith, and it needs space in which to exercise and develop. God comes to us and endows us with the gift of grace so we might know *who* it is that values and cares for us unconditionally. But then we must let go of God's hand and exercise our spiritual muscle in order to get a focus on the promise he holds out to us.

Courage is the empowerment to move toward that which has personal value. Taking the kind of risk that enables us to move into unknown territory for values we believe in is a courageous act. Like a thread running through the Bible is the theme of promise. For Abraham, it was the promised land that required great faith—the leaving behind of kin and country and facing many disappointments and danger. For the Israelites coming out of Egypt, the promise was before them of a land "flowing with milk and honey." Their departure from Egypt and their journey through the wilderness required courage, for God always kept some space between them and his promise, though he also was near enough to answer their call and catch them if they should fall. "Be strong and courageous" was God's command to Joshua and Joshua's to the people (Josh. 1:6, 7, 9).

Courage only exists when there is a space to be crossed in order to receive the promise. "I go to prepare a place for you," Jesus told his disciples, "that where I am, there you may be also" (John 14:2–3). We live in that space between the new life given to us by the Spirit of Jesus and the "place" that is being prepared for us. Meanwhile, living in that space, like the apostle Paul, we throw our heart over the wall and find courage to follow after it (Acts 9:25–26). When Paul found his work virtually completed in Asia Minor, he had a vision one night in which he saw and heard a man from Macedonia calling to him, "Come over . . . and help us" (Acts 16:9). Immediately, Paul found "courage in God," as he liked to put it, and set out for this new land.

I believe that compelling vision would come to each one of us if we were to allow enough space between ourselves and God. What keeps us from an overriding vision and clear focus for our life is not that God is too remote but that we keep him bound to our fear. God is the neighbor, both near and far, if we are willing to see. God will step back, if we will let him, in order to make the vision clear and place our life in focus.

Courage is not so extraordinary for those who have the vision and the focus, and their fears on a leash. Though courage requires something extraordinary from us, this is what makes life a sparkling gem!

4

Compassion

Showing Mercy without Condoning Wrong

Be kind to one another, tenderhearted, forgiving one another, as God in Christ has forgiven you.

Ephesians 4:32

"We should love the sinner but hate the sin," intoned the T.V. evangelist with a smile when asked his opinion of a well-known person who was caught in a sexual impropriety. Was this a demonstration of compassion or thinly veiled contempt? I am not sure. The saying is a familiar one and appears to be a convenient response to the difficult question of how one can sit in judgment of another person's actions without appearing to reject the person. I suspect that the saying is intended as much (or more) to defend the virtue of the one who utters it as it is intended to extend mercy and compassion to the "sinner." I doubt that anyone who has been the object of such a saying has been warmed and encouraged by it!

Jesus did not call anyone a sinner due to their specific moral or spiritual lapses. Those who were called sinners by others, Jesus received with no strings attached. In so doing, he offered them the grace of forgiveness and restoration to a life of holiness and health. So, did he extend compassion at the price of condoning wrong? We shall see.

What Is Compassion?

Compassion is a virtue that we admire in others. None of us would be comfortable if others were to say that we lacked compassion. But what is it?

Is compassion the feeling that some have for whatever appears to be a victim of misfortune, whether it be a wounded bird, a lost dog, or a homeless person who sleeps in the park? Is compassion the indiscriminate expression of sympathy unfettered by moral judgment? Is compassion an alternative to judgment and so to be preferred to the legalistic application of the law?

What is it that we admire in others when we consider it a virtue to be compassionate?

The temptation to view compassion as a gift permits us to admire it in others while settling for something less in ourselves. Compassion is not like musical talent or a special aptitude with mechanical things. It is not a virtue reserved for saints like Mother Teresa. Instead, it is a quality we must cultivate. Inability to demonstrate compassion is a spiritual deficit that betrays a missing piece of our own humanity.

Compassion cultivated and strong becomes an instinctive reaction to the plight of another. We are born with the need for compassion just as surely as we are hungry for our mother's milk and anxious for our father's approval. The need for compassion is also the source of compassion.

The golden rule is just one example. "In everything do to others as you would have them do to you" (Matt. 7:12).

People who are compassionate listen with the "third ear," as someone once said of a good therapist. Normally, we trust the five senses, especially hearing and seeing. People who are intuitive often are said to have a "sixth sense," that of a deeper perception of reality that lies beneath the surface of what is seen and heard.

Keen intuition does not always indicate compassion, though compassionate people probably are also intuitive. People who have compassion look at the same world as others, but they see and care for more than meets the eye.

Let me explain it this way. We cannot see what we do not feel. We cannot care for what we do not see. And we cannot feel what we do not hear.

When Jesus stopped and responded to those who called out to him for help amidst the crowd, it was because he heard their cry. He then responded with compassion. He listened below the tumult and noise of the crowd with the "third ear" and then felt with (com-passion) those who were otherwise invisible to even his disciples.

Matthew records the incident where two blind men called out to him from the large crowd as he was leaving Jericho. The crowd ordered them to be quiet, but "Jesus stood still and called them. . . . Moved with compassion, Jesus touched their eyes. Immediately they regained their sight and followed him" (Matt. 20:32–34).

The Greek word translated as *compassion* literally means *intestines.* The King James Version of the New Testament translates the word quite literally as "bowels of compassion" (1 John 3:17; Phil. 1:8).

The "third ear" with which Jesus sensed the pain of others was the visceral reaction that registered in his own body as he heard and caught sight of all forms of human disorder and distortion.

Compassion

People who have compassion really see the whole picture when they hear the story because they experience for themselves the feeling of despair, loneliness, pain, and burden of guilt that others carry. It was not only on the cross that Jesus "bore our burden" of sin. He was "moved with compassion" on every occasion when confronted by the inhuman burdens others bore and took upon himself their plight and pain.

People who are compassionate cross boundaries in order to help those in need. The boundaries of race, ethnicity, social class, religion, and even moral scruples, are always a challenge to the expression of compassion. Compassionate people dare to cross such boundaries, even though such actions may be a scandal to others.

When the prodigal son returned, according to the parable of Jesus, "while he was still far off, his father saw him and was filled with compassion; he ran and put his arms around him and kissed him" (Luke 15:20). The elder brother was offended by this action and reminded his father of the outrageous and immoral behavior of his younger brother. We admire the virtue of compassion in the father precisely because he crossed over the boundary set by the elder brother.

Jesus was often accused of violating the boundaries religious authorities held to be virtually sacred. When confronted on the sabbath by a man with a paralyzed arm, he had compassion and healed the man. This resulted in the accusation that Jesus was a sabbath breaker and worthy of death. Mark adds the telling comment, "He was grieved at their hardness of heart" (Mark 3:5).

On one accession Jesus was invited to the home of a Pharisee. A woman in the city, "who was a sinner," entered and began to wash his feet with her tears and dry them with her hair. In what must have been a tone dripping with self-righteousness, the host said: "If this man were a prophet, he would have known who and what kind of woman this is who is touching him—that she is a sinner" (Luke 7:39). Again, Jesus had crossed a boundary and received her ministry to him with tenderness and appreciation and replied: "Her sins, which were many, have been forgiven; hence she has shown great love" (Luke 7:47).

We only need to remember the parable of the good Samaritan (Luke 10) to find another instance of a compassionate man who crossed the boundary of race and religion to offer comfort and help to a victim of highway brutality. What marks compassion from mere pity is that compassion leads to action and crosses boundaries to reach the side of those whose lives have been distorted, tormented, and even without moral or religious standing in the community.

Does Compassion Condone Wrongdoing?

In crossing boundaries, does compassion condone wrongdoing? There is a further dimension to compassion that may help us find the answer.

People who are compassionate have a sense of the tragic. For example, a person who acquires AIDS, either through indiscriminate sexual encounter or through a contaminated needle used for a drug injection, has suffered a consequence far beyond a simple penalty for wrongdoing. A jail term, fine, or other penalty would not strike a compassionate person with the same force as the loss of life to such a devastating disease. What some people might dismiss as punishment well deserved, the compassionate person senses as tragic and offers support in the name of common humanity.

If there are persons so evil that their actions lack any semblance of humanity, then we should probably feel moral outrage rather than compassion. Human compassion is not blind and does not blur the distinction between outright evil and distorted humanity. To attribute all evil to social deprivation and not hold individuals responsible for their actions is not compassion but moral naiveté.

The essence of the tragic is a collision between two or more values in real life where no single answer is the right one. The moral issues in life are layered and complex. Choices sometimes have to be made, and failure to act due to moral uncertainty may itself constitute betrayal of the human bond that unites us. The compassionate person is prepared to enter into the arena of the tragic in order to uphold human life in situations where the simple good is not possible.

The moralist avoids the tragic by taking a stand on moral principle as a protection against having to make the most difficult real life choices. The German philosopher Goethe expressed the nature of the tragic in the dialogue in which Pylades tries to persuade Iphigenia to overcome the inner law and still act responsibly:

Pylades
An over-strict demand is secret pride.
Iphigenia
The spotless heart alone is satisfied.
Pylades
Here in the temple you no doubt were so;
And yet life teaches us to be less strict
With others and ourselves; you too will learn,
This human kind is intricately wrought
With knots and ties so manifold that none
Within himself or with the rest can keep
Himself quite disentangled and quite pure.
We are not competent to judge ourselves;
Man's first and foremost duty is to go
Forward and think about his future course:
For he can seldom know what he has done,
And what he now is doing even less . . .
One sees that you have rarely suffered loss;
For if that were not so you would not now
Refuse this one false word to escape this evil.

Iphigenia
Would my heart like a man's could be resolved
And then be deaf to any other voice![1]

By accepting the terms of the tragic, persons with compassion admit that life is far from perfect and that much of the misfortune that comes is due to our own moral failure. This truth can make even responsible action tragic. The compassionate person is not able to satisfy the strict demands of abstract moral law and, at the same time, come to the side of those who are either victims or who are violators of that same law. One can only claim to be perfectly righteous in a legal sense by closing one's ears to the cry of the unrighteous—to be "deaf to any other voice," as Goethe put it. But this choice makes compassion in tragic situations impossible.

The Moral Virtue of Mercy

Compassion is only a feeling until it becomes an act of mercy. In showing mercy, a compassionate person seeks to alleviate pain, temper justice, and restore relationships. Mercy is the fulfillment of compassion and consists in promoting the value of a needy human life when the person least deserves it. We applaud acts of mercy because we recognize the moral goodness of such actions that go beyond the strict demands of the law.

While some people show no mercy because they have no compassion, others who have deep feelings of compassion are reluctant to extend mercy for fear of undermining justice. For some, punishment for violation of either a natural, civil, or divine law is in itself a moral requirement of the law. To release one from the consequences of breaking the law is considered a violation of moral law.

The morality of mercy, on the other hand, is grounded in the character of God and the unconditional love that he extends to humans created in the divine image. In precise terms, forgiveness has to do with release from punishment, not exemption from the law. Mercy is shown to those who have no power or right to establish their own righteousness and well-being. Mercy is a moral demand while forgiveness is not. We cannot force people to forgive when they have been sinned against, but we can expect them to show mercy where it is appropriate. Where forgiveness is offered, mercy has preceded it and constitutes the moral basis for forgiving.

What we admire in persons who show compassion is really the quality of mercy that is demonstrated in their crossing over boundaries to take up the cause of those who have no power or right to restore their own lives. Yet, the very crossing over of boundaries, especially those of a moral or religious nature, can appear to condone wrongdoing in the eyes of some.

The issue of assisted suicide has created a flurry of moral and legal arguments in the state of Michigan. A medical doctor argues that his assistance is within the moral mandate of his oath as a physician to alleviate pain and suffering. In other words, he claims that to provide assistance to a person whose life has become so tormented and painful from incurable illness that the individual chooses to die is an act of mercy. He reasons that the same mercy by which society permits the putting to death of an animal who has suffered irreparable injury ought to apply in the case of humans as well.

For others, the dreadful implications of ending human life at the whim of another or at one's own impulse form a clear moral basis for rejecting such actions as the first step down a "slippery slope" that is without moral restraint and from which there is no hope of return. Fearing such consequences, the doctor's opponents resort to civil law as the only moral check and seek to imprison him as punishment for the crime of assisted suicide.

Meanwhile, physicians across the country quietly report that in a case by case situation, with family consent, they administer medication to terminally ill patients so as to facilitate a speedy death as an alternative to hopeless, prolonged, and painful suffering. They would claim to be acting mercifully though in violation of the law.

Compassion, I have said, has a sense of the tragic, and where values collide in real life situations, many choose to act in mercy rather than to refuse to become involved. If the doctor in Michigan is finally judged guilty and sent to prison, will there be any who would ask for mercy on his behalf? And, if justice prevails, the law is upheld, and his actions are stopped, will that eliminate the need for mercy for other terminally ill persons whose lives have become unbearable? Or is Goethe's Iphigenia correct in her desire for clarity: "Would my heart like a man's could be resolved—And then be deaf to any other voice!"

This case has been cited because it dramatically underscores the tension between justice and mercy, while illustrating that there is often no perfect resolution. While it is true that a society of largely unjust laws, and thus a deficiency of justice, is a great evil, it is also true that a society based on law, but with no capacity to show mercy, is not friendly to human life. Who of us, after all, would be ready to settle for justice when we really need mercy? In the end (or in the beginning!), what is it that causes us to praise God, his justice or his mercy?

The original covenant promise given to Israel was grounded on the mercy of God. The ark of the covenant, which represented the place of atonement, was called the "mercy seat" (Exod. 25:17, 22). God displayed his goodness before Moses and said, "I will be gracious to whom I will be gracious, and will show mercy on whom I will show mercy" (Exod. 33:19). In fact, the mercy of God is grounded in his justice, as Isaiah reports: "Therefore the LORD waits to be gracious to you; therefore he will rise up to show mercy to you. For the LORD is a God of justice; blessed are all those who wait for him" (Isa. 30:18). When the people broke God's law and rebelled against him, they suffered the consequences, yet received his mercy. "Foreigners shall build up your walls, and their kings shall minister to you; for in my wrath I struck you down, but in my favor I have had mercy on you" (Isa. 60:10).

"Blessed are the merciful, for they will receive mercy" (Matt. 5:7), taught Jesus. He practiced what he preached. When confronted by the Pharisees who demanded that he invoke the law of Moses and put to death the woman caught in the act of adultery, he refused to condemn her; but showing mercy, he released her and said, "Go your way, and from now on do not sin again" (John 8:11). After telling the parable of the good Samaritan Jesus asked: "'Which . . . was a neighbor to the man who fell into the hands of the robbers?' He said, 'The one who showed him mercy.' Jesus said to him, 'Go and do likewise'" (Luke 10:36–37).

The inability to show compassion and express mercy is a spiritual deficit and a missing piece of our humanity. Because we are created in the image of God, mercy is a moral virtue of our humanity and a mark of true spiritual maturity. We can strengthen our ability to show mercy by practicing these basic principles.

- Work to grasp the whole picture when listening to or hearing about someone who is caught in a situation that causes pain, powerlessness, or distress. Listen with the "third ear" and hear what is not said. Identify the feelings the other person might have.
- Suspend moral judgment until the moral issues are discerned. A jury is warned not to conduct deliberations or come to conclusions until all of the evidence is in. Often, lack of compassion and the failure to express mercy are due to premature moral judgment about another's situation.

- Compassion is the feeling of being with or alongside someone in need. Imagine another person's circumstance and describe the form mercy would take if it were something you needed in that situation.
- Practice showing mercy in everyday life to those with whom you live and work. Keep a journal of your acts of mercy and describe the effect in each case, both on others and on yourself.

Showing mercy brings its own reward. Opportunities to show mercy occur daily. In place of the slogan "Perform a random act of kindness each day," practice this maxim: "Perform a purposeful act of mercy whenever it is within your power to ease the burden of another's life."

Don't forget to show a little mercy toward yourself!

5

Generosity

Giving Freely
without Giving Yourself Away

Every generous act of giving, with every perfect gift, is from
above, coming down from the Father of lights, with whom there
is no variation or shadow due to change.

James 1:17

Generosity is not a trait one finds in the nature of
things. Oh, there are puppies that slobber their affection
indiscriminately on all who come near. And the warm
breezes of summer sweep over the tender plants that grew
from April showers, as careless in squandering their caresses
as are the flowers in lavishing their fragrance. The harsh
and merciless cold winds of winter are equally as careless
and unrelenting. But these are not examples of generosity.
Some things just overflow by their very nature.

Nor should one mistake the animal instinct for feeding and caring for its young as generosity. The mother cat that carries a freshly caught bird, dripping with blood, to be devoured by the ravenous hunger of her kittens is not willing to share her catch with another of her own kind, no matter how desperate the need. Once the kittens have become grown cats, they will have to compete with the one who gave them life in order to survive. We must look beyond these basic instincts to find the spirit of generosity.

Nor is generosity so natural to humans. Here too we find instincts and impulses to share with and care for our own—up to a point! Most parents will give their children more generous helpings than they take for themselves when there is a scarcity of food. But some of the same parents will jealously guard and hoard their resources from their adult children out of fear that they will not have enough to care for themselves. Is it a lack of confidence in the generosity of their own children that causes this compulsive clutching? Or is it that what once appeared as generosity was only a duty?

That generosity is a virtue we admire is evidence that it does not come naturally. When we encounter truly generous persons, or are fortunate enough to live with or be related to such, we recognize generosity to be a virtue. Nor do we have to be the recipients of generosity to admire the virtue of generosity in others. Like a yellow daisy growing amidst the clutter of a vacant lot, the spirit of a generous person sends a signal that humanity can rise above its propensity to selfishness in order to shine upon us.

The Profile of a Generous Spirit

Generosity is not only a virtue, it is a fruit of the Spirit (Gal. 5:23). Not every act of benevolence has its source in a spirit of generosity. Some do good as a way of gaining the praise and approval of others. Others give gifts that have strings attached and that are meant to gain some future advantage or to create an obligation to reciprocate.

One reason we admire true generosity as a virtue in others is the absence of a spirit of retaliation when offended.

When Joe spread the word around the rural village that Charlie, his neighbor, had taken one of Joe's cows and sold it along with a truckload he had recently shipped to market, there was an uproar in the community. Charlie was denounced from the pulpit in one church and trounced in the local paper by a scathing editorial. A few weeks later, to Joe's chagrin, someone discovered his missing cow wandering loose in another part of the county. He wrote a letter to the editor of the local paper acknowledging his false charge and then approached Charlie fully expecting to be met with anger. To his surprise, Charlie extended his hand and said, "Well, Joe, you got your cow back and that is all that really matters. After all, we are neighbors and have to get along the best we can."

"That is mighty generous of you," Joe responded. "I don't know if I would be so forgiving if I were in your place."

In this case, the spirit of generosity demonstrated by Charlie was recognized as a virtue because he did not exercise what many would have considered his right to be angry and exact some recompense from Joe as a matter of justice. The absence of a spirit of retaliation in Charlie was acknowledged by Joe as being "mighty generous."

Something else that makes generosity a virtue we admire in others is the lack of a spirit of impatience when demands are made upon it that take additional time and effort. The beggar who asks for money is not nearly as troublesome for many of us as those who ask of us additional time and effort due to their own incompetence, poor planning, or even misfortune. But a truly generous spirit will lack impatience in either case.

"I hate to ask for additional time to turn in my term paper," came the plaintive voice of a student over the telephone. "I know that the paper is due tomorrow, but my computer crashed as I was writing it, and I have to start all over on it." I did not probe into the reasons why the student had delayed writing the paper until the night before it was due. I have taught long enough to know that the habit of procrastination comes with a glossary of excuses.

"My grades are due a week from Monday," I replied. "If you can get your paper to me by next Friday, I will read it over the weekend and turn in your grade. I am sorry that you have lost all of your work. Don't panic; take your time and do it well." I veiled my impatience with the student for not having guarded against computer crash panic by making a backup copy of the file on which he had been working. I made a mental note to save time the following weekend to read the paper and ended the conversation. I am no longer surprised by such intrusions and accept them as part of the teaching contract.

What did surprise me was the note from the student when the paper was graded and returned. The student lauded my generosity effusively. I had to stop and think. The grade awarded was rather mediocre, accurately reflecting the quality of the paper. No generosity there! What I perceived as an accommodation to the student in bending the rules and making an exception was viewed by the student as generosity on my part. I felt a little guilty, because my feelings of impatience were real, though concealed from him. The student had made an intrusion into my time requiring extra effort—an intrusion I felt would have been unnecessary had he planned his work more effectively, leaving time for unforeseen emergencies such as computer failure. If the student suspected that I had feelings of impatience, he nevertheless regarded as generous my willingness to work out an arrangement by which he could complete his work.

In reflecting upon this incident, I discovered that the proof of generosity lies in the perception that others have of us, not in our own self-perception. Regardless of what we may intend, an action is probably not generous until it is perceived as such by others. Furthermore, I learned that what is viewed as generosity is really behavior that elevates the common bond of shared human experience over claims for what we think is ours alone.

"After all," Charlie told Joe, "we are neighbors and have to get along the best we can." I doubt that Charlie felt very generous at the time, but Joe perceived his response as such. They shared a common bond that took precedence over retaliation and resentment. The student sensed a common bond of human concern that took precedence over the rules and regulations that deprived him of his needs but gave me the right to fail him for the course. He interpreted my willingness to bend the rules and accept the request as generosity.

The virtue of generosity is a sharing of the human spirit in the face of conditions that tend to isolate and alienate us. Distrust of a neighbor led Joe to accuse Charlie of theft, when he had no evidence. The rift created cut right through the heart of the community and threatened the common bond on which their survival depended. A year earlier when Joe was hospitalized at harvest time, his neighbors, Charlie included, had stopped their own harvest to spend a day harvesting all of his crops.

When Charlie told Joe, "We are neighbors and have to get along the best we can," he was reminding him that their only hedge against misfortune and failure was a common commitment to each other's welfare. While they did not hold their farms and property in common, they held their life in common. When we recognize and mourn the loss of such values in our own society, we make a mistake if we think that the spirit of generosity exhibited in this case is an artifact of a rural community. The generosity that issues from a shared sense of life is not a value unique to rural community but an essential aspect of living in any human community.

When the early Christians gathered to form a new community following the day of Pentecost, Luke tells us that "they broke bread at home and ate their food with glad and generous hearts" (Acts 1:46). As the need arose, they shared even their possessions with each other. "Now the whole group of those who believed were of one heart and soul, and no one claimed private ownership of any possessions, but everything they owned was held in common. . . . There was not a needy person among them, for as many as owned lands or houses sold them and brought the proceeds of what was sold" (Acts 4:32, 34). The fact was that some did own property and had right of disposal over it, as Luke also makes clear (5:4).

The spirit of generosity was evident first of all in their "one heart and soul." While some did own property, they did not "claim" private ownership. That is, they did not claim ownership of property as an absolute right. The common life that they shared conditioned their right to keep what was their own while others went hungry.

The spirit of generosity is the spirit of a shared life, where a teacher's prerogatives are conditioned by a student's predicament. For a teacher to define his life solely by the prerogatives that limit his relationship to another person as a "student" is to narrow the relationship and empty it of human meaning. Without a sense of shared humanity, there will be no generosity and little virtue.

Why Generosity Is a Spiritual Virtue

Those who lack the virtue of generosity suffer a spiritual deficit. Their own spirit is cramped and crushed, like an eagle caged in a zoo. Lacking the freedom to soar, its spirit turns sour and surly. Stalking the boundaries of its limited existence, the unfree spirit misinterprets the freedom of others as prodigality and becomes miserly and mean. It is the meanness of spirit, not the habit of miserliness, that marks the spiritual deficit in the ungenerous. Fearing the bonding of spirit with another as a form of bondage, those who lack the spirit of generosity retaliate when they are wounded and are impatient with the suffering of others. The ungenerous spirit maintains its freedom from the demands of others by cutting the cords of human compassion and declaring its own resident alien status in the human family.

When Ed was injured in a construction accident, he drew disability through workman's compensation until it was determined that he was no longer eligible. His brother, Paul, and sister, Diane, were full partners along with Ed in the family construction business they had inherited from their father. Paul decided that Ed should continue to draw a salary from the company even though he could not work on the building sites and had no experience in office work, which Diane handled by herself. A conflict arose between Paul and Diane over Ed's situation, and she refused to accept Paul's decision to provide this financial assistance to Ed. When they could not resolve this within the family, Diane engaged an attorney and filed suit, seeking to dissolve the partnership, leaving Ed with only a modest financial settlement and no future income.

When Ed shared his story with his pastor, he lamented the loss of relationship with his sister and the destructive nature of the legal action upon the family. "I have no argument with the financial settlement," he said. "I have no right to expect more than my fair share of what little equity we have in the business. What disturbs me the most is the fact that my sister could be so mean to me. She has a streak of meanness that I have never seen before."

As long as they each were healthy and productive, the two brothers and their sister maintained the semblance of being partners and family. Generosity may have been given in small ways, for there was no great need among them. Ed's injury and incapacitation snapped the fragile bond in that family system and exposed the spiritual deficit in Diane. Reacting instinctively, she sought legal recourse to eliminate the claim that her position as Ed's sister laid upon her to share his misfortune. What Ed lamented far more than the loss of his own productive capacity was the discovery of what he called meanness in his sister.

The lack of a spirit of generosity in another is far more than a personality trait. It is an attack on the spirit of common life that binds us together in the tenuous task of living humanly and gracefully amidst the "slings and arrows of outrageous fortune," as Shakespeare put it.

Generosity is not measured by random acts of giving but through consistent readiness to recognize and preserve the common bond of shared life. A generous person will always be prepared to give, even if nothing can be given. One cannot give what one does not have. But one can always be ready and eager to give.

Generosity is not only an extraordinary virtue to be admired in saints; it is the very essence of the bonding of the human spirit to its fellows. Benevolent actions flow out of the virtue of generosity. The motive for the giving of one's money, time, and resources to meet the needs of others is rooted in the spirit of generosity. One can live without the spirit of generosity, but no one can be spiritually fit without this spirit. It is a law of life.

The Law of Generosity

Generosity is not only a virtue; it is a law of life grounded in the fact that humans bear the image and likeness of a God who has breathed his own Spirit into our mortal bodies (Gen. 2:7). The spirit of generosity is a mark of spiritual maturity and balance, and it contributes to the health and well-being of one's whole life.

When Jesus spoke of generosity, he left little room to squirm away. "Give to everyone who begs from you, and do not refuse anyone who wants to borrow from you" (Matt. 5:42). By this Jesus meant that we should seek by all possible means to respond to another's request for aid. Paul spells this out in practical terms: "For if the eagerness is there, the gift is acceptable according to what one has—not according to what one does not have" (2 Cor. 8:12).

What Paul calls the "eagerness" to give is the spirit of generosity as I have described it above. "Each of you must give as you have made up your mind, not reluctantly or under compulsion, for God loves a cheerful giver" (2 Cor. 9:7). Generosity is a perception other people have of our own eagerness and readiness to affirm the common bond that unites our human life.

Is there a limit to our giving? Is there a virtue in giving so much that one no longer has anything left to give? Can we give freely without giving ourselves away?

There are certainly limits. In extending the deadline for the student's paper, I set a limit based on my own deadline. I live under certain constraints, and it is only within those constraints that I can demonstrate an "eagerness to give." The student apparently interpreted my extension within these limits as an unqualified generous act—even though the terms of the contract were clear and binding. This was more than he had a right to expect, but all that he hoped for!

When Charlie shook hands with Joe and dismissed the damage done to his reputation for the sake of maintaining the bond of being good neighbors, Joe found that action to be "mighty generous." It was more than he had a right to expect, but all that he had hoped for! At the same time, in binding Joe to the contractual terms of being a good neighbor, Charlie set limits that Joe must respect and honor. In his perception of the generosity of Charlie, Joe had no right to continue to abuse the good name of his neighbor. Nor would he have claimed that right.

The spirit of generosity is always present within limits. We do not admire a person who squanders his entire fortune nor gives away that which is the source of his own livelihood. We call such people fools, not role models for generosity.

Not only is generosity always within certain constraints but it also functions in a reciprocal context. The law of generosity presupposes the possibility of reciprocity. No person lives totally unto himself. "No man is an island," the poet John Donne reminded us. "Good fences make good neighbors," Robert Frost's neighbor opined. But Frost responded, "Before I built a wall, I'd ask to know what I was walling in or walling out."

Ed accepted the fact that the financial settlement of the partnership was fair. He did not expect his sister Diane to give away all that she had to support him. He understood there were limits, but he hoped for a spirit of generosity within those constraints. Her resort to legal action was perceived to be mean-spirited because it built a wall between them through which their spirits could not pass.

The spirit of generosity respects the integrity of others but leaves room in the wall for mutual exchange of life. The measure we give is the measure that we receive in return.

"Give, and it will be given to you," said Jesus. "A good measure, pressed down, shaken together, running over, will be put into your lap; for the measure you give will be the measure you get back" (Luke 6:38). Paul adds: "The point is this: the one who sows sparingly will also reap sparingly, and the one who sows bountifully will also reap bountifully" (2 Cor. 9:6).

The spirit of generosity is a law of human life. It is the bond that preserves human dignity and value amidst the dehumanizing and depersonalizing forces of everyday life. Generosity is a virtue that we admire in others because we long for the recovery of mutual care as a spiritual value of human life.

It is not necessary for us to think of ourselves as generous, though it is wise to do so. It is sufficient to extend ourselves beyond what is our right in order to create a space for others to live. Generosity is a virtue perceived in us by others as we go beyond what is expected and give what is hoped for.

The Spiritual Fruit of Generosity

To manifest the spirit of generosity is to go beyond what is fair and cause life to become fruitful. Generosity is a fruit of the Spirit. Spiritual balance produces the fruit of generosity through creative actions that enhance the lives of others.

We produce the spiritual fruit of generosity when we live in the creative space between the outer limit and the inner circle of our life. Each of us has an inner circle of self-interest and self-preservation. The outer limit is the bond of mutual interest and mutual preservation that bring certain constraints upon our life. The outer limit should never be identical with this inner circle. Generosity is the creative gift that creates mutual life and blessing between the inner circle and the outer limit.

When one is driving a car with children as passengers, the outer limit is represented by the responsibility for safe arrival at the proper time and destination. The inner limit is represented by the self-interest of the adult who has control of the car. The one who has control of the wheel has the right to determine the direction and speed. To give over the wheel and control of the car to a child who asks to drive would be irresponsible and would be to "give away" one's own life as well as the lives of others in the car. But the inner circle of self-interest and control on the part of the driver is not identical with the outer limit. The outer limit is the constraint upon the driver to deliver the passengers safely at the appointed destination. Given certain variables in time and circumstance, there may be some creative space between the inner circle of control and the outer limit of constraint.

There is room for a spirit of generosity as a creative gift when a child wishes to stop and explore a point of interest. Having control of the steering wheel gives one certain "rights" in determining where the car should go. One may not expect the driver to change course and allow for the whim of the child, but the child can *hope* for this! And if this hope is realized, the driver will be perceived as "mighty generous"! This assumes, of course, that safe arrival at the appointed destination in reasonable time occurs! Sometimes, even the destination and time are negotiable if there is the spirit of generosity. My point is that there is often some room between the outer limit of constraint upon us and the inner circle of our own self-interest.

The illustration can be changed slightly to include adults who "go along for the ride" but then wish to make an unplanned stop. Here too the one who controls the car has an inner circle of personal self-interest along with the outer limit of constraints as to time and destination. Within these two, there is negotiable space for the intrusion of desires and wishes where the spirit of generosity may respond. We have all ridden or been with people who operate only on the basis of the inner circle and whose life is non-negotiable with regard to the creation of space for generosity. Without speaking of it in so many words, we experience such people as mean and narrow, ungenerous and unaware of the pain they cause.

In reflection upon the case with my student, the inner circle was my right to hold the student accountable to the original deadline, even if that meant failure for the student. The outer limit was the constraint upon me to turn in my grades at a certain date. The ten days' time that separated these points of reference was the space in which a creative response could be given without violating the outer limit. The student had no right to expect or claim this space but could hope for it. When it was given and received, it was perceived by the student as generosity on my part. I could give freely without giving myself away.

It is appropriate for us to claim control over certain aspects of our life as it intersects with other people. Being in control, we have certain rights—this is the inner circle. We can defend our rights at this point against the wishes and needs of others. But the outer limit is not identical with this inner circle. There is always some space where a creative gift of life can be given. Being in control does not mean that we cannot explore the space that exists up to the outer circle of constraint.

We can grow in the spirit of generosity through an exercise in which we define the space between our inner circle of self-interest and the outer circle of constraint in each of our relationships. In some cases, the space will be rather small; in other cases we will be amazed to discover how much room there is to negotiate and produce the spiritual fruit of generosity.

The law of generosity will then come into play: "The one who sows sparingly will also reap sparingly, and the one who sows bountifully will also reap bountifully" (2 Cor. 9:6). Sowing the seeds of generosity in the creative space between us and the other person produces a fruitful garden from which we both eat freely.

6

Kindness

Taking Care
without Taking Control

You remember our labor and toil, brothers and sisters; we worked night and day, so that we might not burden any of you while we proclaimed to you the gospel of God.

1 Thessalonians 2:9

Random acts of kindness are like rainbows that arch across the stormy sky while the raindrops are still falling. They catch us by surprise, startle us with their brilliance, but disappear as suddenly as they come.

Being waved into a space in the crowded parking lot at the mall by someone who had first chance at it is a stunning exception to what we expect and to our own practice! We may speculate for a few minutes about what prompted this rare expression of kindness by a perfect stranger. But such a random act of kindness is a virtue doomed to anonymity and is filed under "miscellaneous." Even a rainbow can be captured on film, but kindness without a name or face is only a story without a plot. Anecdotes are no antidote for a life without regular doses of intentional care.

While kindness brightens the day, it is care that touches the heart. Care is more than random kindness, it is loving kindness.

Eavesdropping on Adam and Eve

"I know you love me; but do you really care for me?"

It was a troubling question; he paused before attempting an answer. *There must be a catch to it,* he thought to himself. It was the kind of question that was like picking up a poisonous snake. If he took it by the tail it would turn and bite him. And if he tried for the head, it would strike before he could get a good grip on it.

"I thought loving meant caring," he ventured, hoping to buy some time and gain a piece of open road so that he could see what lay ahead.

Instead, she took a hard left turn that left him slightly disoriented. "Adam, do you remember the conversation we had last evening at dinner with the Smiths?"

"Sure," he responded, a bit too quickly, and was immediately worried that he had appeared relieved at the change of subject. "We were talking about the vacation trip we took last month to Maui. I remember telling Julie how great you looked in your bathing suit."

"That wasn't exactly how you put it," she responded carefully, as though measuring her words before she spoke in order to place them in their proper order. "You said it to Jim, not Julie, and what you actually said was, 'Eve worried about going to Maui and wearing a bathing suit because she has put on a lot of weight. But I told her not to worry, because she always looks great to me. The more the better!'"

He was relieved. *So that was all that she was worried about.* Smiling, he said, "Didn't I say you looked great? I thought you would take that as a compliment."

"You probably didn't notice that I got up and left the table at that point. You were laughing with Jim as though it were some kind of joke. I felt so humiliated! But I don't think that you really care how I feel."

Suddenly he had a sinking feeling. She was in one of those moods again. He knew now that nothing he could say would help, and if he tried it would only get worse.

He couldn't let it go, of course. "You think I don't care about you?" He realized that his voice had taken on an edge. Speaking more softly and reaching out to take her hand, he said, "I knew that you were tired after teaching school all year and I thought that you needed to get away. That is why I wanted to surprise you with a trip to Maui."

"Did you ask me first? You think that taking over my life is caring?"

"I'm going out for a while," he said. "We can talk about this later if you want."

When Taking Care May Not Be Caring

The pathos in the above scenario seeps through the conversation like an unhealed wound seeps through its gauze wrapping. Perhaps if she bleeds enough the pain will jump-start the collapsed heart of a love that no longer beats. Her feelings protrude like tender green shoots on a well-worn path, only to be crushed in the foot traffic of aimless words. She knows where he walks, and her only hope is to cause him to stumble, even if it means her suffering another bruise.

Behind the confusion and uncertainty of his unsuccessful groping toward a rational handhold in the conversation there lurks the startled response of a deer caught in the headlights. The fear is palpable. There is terror in his heart. One false move and he will be roadkill on the highway of love.

Lest I be charged with being overly dramatic, I remind the reader that no relation is so likely to cause abuse and no encounter so potentially cruel as one that begins with the promise of love. To love and be loved is to experience the highest value that life can offer. It is also to risk the greatest pain and loss that life can bring. When we love, we need to take care. We cannot drive a car without passing a test to gain a license, but we can become a parent and begin a marriage with a $50 fee and a promise of love. Careless drivers who cause injury are removed from the road. Careless lovers wound their children for life and make their bed in the wreckage of a ruined relationship.

These are two people who became careless with the promise of love. Without care, love is unkind, even cruel. Nor is taking care of another the same as really caring. We want to be cared for, not taken care of. The distinction is more than semantic.

I take care of my car because I have a sense of ownership and pride. It also is submissive to my control and subject to my command. We take care of our homes, our pets, and our possessions in the same sense. Taking care *of* something means that we control it, at least to a certain extent. What we take care of tends to become an object of care and subject to our control. When we take care of something in this sense, the object of our care tends to be viewed impersonally. Unless, as some are prone to do, we personify the object of our care, which is really a projection of our own personality upon the object.

When we take care *for* someone, it is the personal life of the other that we care for. Taking care of an infant involves more than providing for its objective needs. The caregiver is also attentive to the feelings, desires, and mystery of personhood that is aroused and affirmed. As the life of a child develops, the controlling aspect of caring is intended to diminish as the child begins to care for herself. Taking care *of* gradually shifts to taking care *for* the personal life of the child growing into an adult. The goal is finally to take care without taking control.

Let us revisit the scenario described above. Adam is confused and threatened over the suggestion that loving is not the same as caring. He feels most tender about the one he takes care of. In taking care of her he feels like he is loving. In the conversation with his friend, Jim, he mentions his wife with the same affection that he might feel toward his ten-year-old car. He probably also calls it "old Bessie" and might say, "She is getting old and has a few dents but with a coat of wax and a tune-up she runs as well as ever. They don't make them like that anymore!"

When he speaks of his wife with the same sentiment, it is with pride of ownership and self-satisfaction in taking good care of her. After all, as he reminded Eve, he sensed that she too needed a "tune-up" and arranged to surprise her with a vacation to Maui.

Her feelings do not register with him. He can only attribute them to "one of those moods again." His way of complimenting her is to "damn her with faint praise." Talking about her as though she were not there, he told Jim, "She has put on a lot of weight. But I told her not to worry, because she always looks great to me. The more the better!" He has the same feelings as standing in the driveway talking about "old Bessie." The fact that his wife felt humiliated and so upset that she left the room simply did not make an impact on him. Even in retrospect, he is unable to connect with her feelings at the time, and even less as she now confronts him. His way of being kind is to take care of something, to always be in control. She experiences this as cruel and uncaring. Love without caring is unkind. Lack of kindness is slowly killing their love.

Kindness, like most other virtues in life, is the effect others have upon us. Only those who come within the circle of our caring can make this judgment. I am not the authority as to whether or not I am kind. Those for whom I care know the truth.

Kindness is an acquired virtue, not an instinctive trait. "Love is kind," wrote the apostle Paul. "It does not insist on its own way" (1 Cor. 13:4–5). Like generosity, kindness is a fruit of the Spirit (Gal. 5:22). One aspect of spiritual fitness is learning to take care without taking control. Kindness is the litmus test of love.

Kindness: The Litmus Test of Love

Lack of kindness is more easily defined than kindness itself. It is not kind to expose another to humiliation or embarrassment. It is not kind to cause unnecessary harm or hurt to someone. It is not kind to be insensitive to the feelings and emotions of another. It is not kind to be rude or to ridicule someone and to treat them impersonally in a personal situation. It is not kind to take advantage of another, either due to their weakness or one's own superior position.

Kindness is not dependent upon intimacy or love, for strangers can be kind, and those with whom we have no relationship often demonstrate this virtue. Love, however, does depend upon kindness, for, as Paul wrote, "love is kind." The reason that love is kind is because it does not act with rudeness and does not harm or hurt another. Kindness is thus a litmus test for love, for the profession of love must include the intention to be kind.

Friendship may be the only form of human social relationship that is sustained primarily by kindness. All other forms of social relationships, such as parent/child, husband/wife, employer/employee, co-worker, neighbor, exist by virtue of extrinsic factors as well as intrinsic qualities. One continues to function as a parent, spouse, worker, and neighbor, even though kindness may be lacking. Though it must also be said that the quality of these functions may become so barren of kindness that they become abusive and intolerable. It is also true that some relationships, such as parent/child and husband/wife, have a greater dependence upon kindness than others.

One can be a good neighbor, a good employee, or employer, and even a good husband or wife as long as "good" means fulfilling one's obligations, without the virtue of kindness. What I mean is that the absence of kindness does not immediately dissolve the form of the relationship, though it may affect the quality of the relationship.

With friendship, it is entirely different. Kindness is the glue that binds friends together. If I should humiliate a friend, be insensitive to the feelings of a friend, cause unnecessary harm or hurt to a friend, or in any way treat a friend as an object that I use for my own pleasure and gratification, the friendship dissolves. There is no reason a person should want to continue a friendship where there is no kindness, unless we are using the friendship to meet other needs. And in that case it is not a true and healthy friendship.

In the scenario with which this chapter began, Adam's lack of kindness was experienced by Eve as insensitivity to her feelings when he made comments about her weight to his friend. She felt humiliated and was hurt by the joke he made. Adam would not have taken the same liberty with his friend Jim, for he would have instinctively sensed the effect of his words as creating a negative reaction. Because intimacy creates massive blind spots, married persons often take the liberty of saying hurtful things to each other and acting toward each other with great rudeness and carelessness. This type of behavior would end a friendship quickly unless there was repentance and forgiveness leading to restoration of the relationship.

Why does it seem easier to show kindness to a friend than to one's marriage partner? When persons who are married do not show kindness as a consistent pattern, the marriage is no longer a caring and loving one. Such a marriage has failed the litmus test of love, for love is not a relationship where one only takes care *of* the other but where both take care *for* the other. When one becomes incapacitated and unable to care for oneself, the other partner's taking care of the incapacitated one becomes the deepest expression of love. The original promise of love includes the commitment to the care of each other physically should the need arise. But mutual care *for* each other is what keeps lovers friends and produces the fruit of kindness.

What is it that prompts kindness in marriage and a friendship, or even the random act of kindness by a stranger? What clues can be found in order to achieve this virtue as a key element of our spiritual maturity?

Clues to Kindness

The first clue as to what prompts kindness was discovered through our discussion of friendship. Friendship is based on mutuality and reciprocity.

• Kindness is *the radar* by which one reads the soul of another person. To make a friend one must demonstrate care for the other person by sensing the other's feelings, needs, desires, and interests. Persons who express kindness have a kind of sixth sense by which they perceive what another feels. Perhaps this requires more spiritual sensitivity than psychic intuition. We are connected to other persons by a human spirit that shares the common essence of the image of God.

When we encounter another at the personal level rather than merely as an object, our own spirit searches out the spirit of the other. Our human spirit is something like a radar beam that sweeps across the landscape of another's soul, detecting the feelings that belong to the personal life of the other. "The human spirit is the lamp of the LORD, searching every inmost part" (Prov. 20:27). When we turn our spirit outward from ourselves and become sensitive to the spirit of others, we have discovered a clue by which we can achieve the virtue of kindness.

- Kindness is *the monitor* that registers the discomfort of others. Adam did not perceive the discomfort of his wife when he made his joking comment to Jim. Her embarrassment and obvious movement to leave the table at that point simply did not register with him. Persons who express kindness see what remains oblivious to others. Their spiritual sensitivity helps them interpret what they see as signals of distress or discomfort in others.

What some may see as intrusive behavior the kind person interprets as a cry for help. On one occasion a woman pressed through the crowd surrounding Jesus and touched the fringe of his clothes. When Jesus asked, "Who touched me?" all denied it and Peter said, "Master, the crowds surround you and press in on you." But Jesus said, "Someone touched me; for I noticed that power had gone out from me." Luke then adds, "When the woman saw that she could not remain hidden, she came trembling; and falling down before him, she declared in the presence of all the people why she had touched him, and how she had been immediately healed" (Luke 8:45–47).

Jesus monitored the discomfort and needs of those around him. This is a clue to the virtue of kindness. We cannot express kindness when the personal life of others remains invisible to us. Kindness begins when the radar of our spirit picks up the feelings and needs of others, and when others register on our perceptive monitor as people who need someone to touch.

- Kindness is *the feedback loop* that connects the response of others to our own words and actions. The maintenance of friendship requires careful discernment of how one's words and actions affect the other person. Discerning the effect of a word or action prior to it being spoken or performed enables one to choose words that project kindness and care. Words that hurt are often the ones spoken thoughtlessly and carelessly. Lack of kindness indicates a broken connection between ourselves and others.

The connection between Adam and Eve, as we observed, was broken. Neither was connected to the other with a feedback loop. Their words not only missed the target, but there was not even the echo of a response. The truth of our words is not only what we intend but also their effect on others.

The apostle Paul describes this perfectly when he says: "But speaking the truth in love, we must grow up in every way into him who is the head, into Christ, from whom the whole body, joined and knit together by every ligament with which it is equipped, as each part is working properly, promotes the body's growth in building itself up in love" (Eph. 4:15–16).

When we are connected to other people through love, there must be mutual interchange so that we are "joined and knit together by every ligament." Kindness is the "ligament" of love. Kindness is what others feel when we draw them toward us, rather than repel them, with our words and actions. To use another metaphor, kindness is the "Achilles tendon" that connects our words to our walk. Often after we have offended someone we say, "I certainly put my foot in my mouth today!" Or, "I could kick myself for saying that!" This is a strange metaphor! But in using it we confess that our words were inappropriate and even offensive. Getting proper feedback and taking responsibility for the effect of our words is a clue by which we can achieve the virtue of kindness.

• Kindness is *the buffer* we place between another and the unfriendly forces and faces in life. When Jesus was confronted by the religious leaders of his day who threw at his feet a woman caught in the act of adultery, he not only uttered a word of forgiveness ("I do not condemn you") but also expressed kindness by presenting himself as a buffer between her and her accusers (see John 8:1–11).

Kindness is the shelter we provide for those exposed to the merciless winds of misfortune. Kindness is the covering we provide for those exposed to the impersonal and inquisitive eyes of the voyeurs who are attracted to the naked folly of others while clothing themselves with self-righteous contempt. Kindness is the shield we provide for the defenseless when under attack by "disputes without and fears within" (2 Cor. 7:5). Kindness is a therapeutic buffer for those suffering emotional and mental distress and a personal buffer for those whose spirit is wounded by the careless words and actions of others.

Eve was in the presence of two other friends, Jim and Julie, when her husband made his joking but cruel remarks. Who cared? No one! Neither Jim nor Julie's radar was working and their monitor was turned off. Nothing registered, or if it did, they swallowed the impulse to become involved. Kindness would have come to the side of Eve, making visible to Adam the effects of his remarks. It is not kind to allow someone like Adam to get away with his insensitive remarks. Nor is it kind to abandon Eve at the moment when she is defenseless and exposed to rudeness and ridicule.

We discover a clue to the virtue of kindness when we ask the question "Who cares?" and respond with "I care."

• Kindness is *the seed we plant* in another's garden to grow fruit for our own enjoyment. When we care for the garden of another's life we are ensuring a harvest of fruit for our own pleasure. The proverb says it well: "Those who are kind reward themselves, but the cruel do themselves harm" (Prov. 11:17).

Kindness is more than altruism, which is a benevolent act without regard for any benefit to the self. Kindness is an investment that pays rich dividends. We are dependent upon the kindness of others when our own life becomes narrow and painful. The folk expression "the milk of human kindness" points to the nourishing aspect of kindness we both receive from others and that we can give to others.

7

Wisdom

Loving Freely without Loving Foolishly

Who is wise and understanding among you? Show by your good life that your works are done with gentleness born of wisdom. ... the wisdom from above is first pure, then peaceable, gentle, willing to yield, full of mercy and good fruits.

James 3:13, 17

Among the book titles in the popular psychology section of many bookstores is one called *Women Who Love Too Much: When You Keep Wishing and Hoping He'll Change.* The impulse behind those who write such books and the readers who buy them is the concern that a compulsive giving of love makes one vulnerable to exploitation and abuse. Those who love freely often end up loving foolishly.

Loving too much, these authors suggest, is one way of becoming a victim by being too open and too vulnerable.

One is susceptible to abuse when loving takes the form of excessive giving of oneself to another. Those who exploit the vulnerability of others are predators; those who succumb are victims.

Children are trusting by nature, because they are open to those who offer care and are defenseless in the face of those who use that openness to seduce and violate them. When our four-year-old grandson was scolded by his mother for talking with a stranger on the street outside their home, the boy replied, "But he wasn't a stranger because he told me his name!"

Teaching our children to be suspicious of strangers while encouraging them to remain open and vulnerable to love is a delicate balance between trust and caution, between loving freely and loving foolishly. Vulnerability is the open window of the heart through which our human spirits can meet and mingle. The closed self suffers a spiritual deficit, for the spirit cannot thrive except when it is nourished by another spirit. The self unwilling to disclose itself is unable to receive the love of others and unable to give love in return. Self-disclosure is the key that unlocks the heart and opens the door to love.

The Wisdom of Vulnerability

Vulnerability is a mark of spiritual fitness that enhances our relationship with one another and with God. Indeed, the self-disclosure of God through Jesus and the Spirit is the language of love, grace, and mercy through which God became vulnerable and accessible.

Jesus is the disclosure of the very heart of God and, as such, is the wisdom of God. "No one has ever seen God. It is God the only Son, who is close to the Father's heart, who has made him known" (John 1:18). Near the end of his life, Jesus told his disciples, "I have made known to you everything that I have heard from my father. . . . When the Spirit of truth comes . . . He will glorify me, because he will take what is mine and declare it to you" (John 15:15; 16:13–14). Jesus became the open window of the heart of God through whom our spirits can meet and mingle with the Spirit of God.

Divine self-disclosure is a virtue of God because it reveals his vulnerability to the human spirit's search for grace, mercy, and love. Tragically, in becoming vulnerable and loving freely, God became the victim of human violence against love when Jesus was put to death on a cross. In claiming to be wise, humans put to death the wisdom of God.

Yet, as Paul says, what appeared as the foolishness of God in loving freely actually revealed the wisdom of God. "For God's foolishness is wiser than human wisdom, and God's weakness is stronger than human strength" (1 Cor. 1:25).

It was the wisdom of God to overcome human violence against love, and through his self-disclosure and self-sacrifice he brought healing and hope, through the resurrection of Christ and the gift of the Spirit. The Spirit of Jesus is the wisdom of God in contrast to the foolishness of the spirit of the world. God loves freely but not foolishly.

The self-disclosure of God is the gift of God and the key to spiritual balance: "For what human being knows what is truly human except the human spirit that is within? So also no one comprehends what is truly God's except the Spirit of God. Now we have received not the spirit of the world, but the Spirit that is from God, so that we may understand the gifts bestowed on us by God" (1 Cor. 2:11–12).

Paul experienced for himself the disclosure of divine mercy and love through the Spirit of Jesus Christ. This revelation transformed Saul of Tarsus from a merciless and violent predator, who hunted down believers in Christ, into Paul, the apostle of love.

When he spoke of his manner of approach in leading others to experience this transforming power of the Spirit, Paul's words were couched in the language of love: "So deeply do we care for you that we are determined to share with you not only the gospel of God but also our own selves, because you have become very dear to us" (1 Thess. 2:8). In expressing gratitude to the church at Philippi for their generous gift he wrote in such personal terms that he appeared to defend his effusive display of feelings: "It is right for me to think this way about all of you, because you hold me in your heart" (Phil. 1:7). Paul loved freely but not foolishly.

Among the other virtues we admire in Paul is his spirit of self-disclosure, which made him vulnerable and accessible to others. This did not come easy for him. His defenses were broken and his hardness of heart overcome by the self-disclosure of Jesus to him through a transforming spiritual encounter. Even then, his reputation followed him, and when he went to Jerusalem to meet with the apostles, they drew back in fear. To them he was still Saul the predator, and none of them wished to become vulnerable to his murderous intentions. It was Barnabas who interceded and disclosed to them the transformation that had taken place so that they came to trust Paul (see Acts 9:26–27). In trusting him, they themselves became vulnerable. But only in becoming vulnerable could they discern the Spirit of the Lord in him.

Not all vulnerability is authentic self-disclosure, however, and love without mutual self-disclosure is not a virtue, nor is it wise. Love without wisdom is not only foolish, it is shaming and destructive.

Vulnerability without Virtue

Women Who Love Too Much is a title sure to catch the attention of those who have become victims of their own vulnerability and who have loved foolishly. The underlying message in the title is that women get hurt when they try to gain love by giving too much and getting back too little. The attempt to use self-disclosure as a means of getting love makes one vulnerable to abuse. The end result is becoming a victim and getting hurt. The attempt to gain love through the giving of oneself in such a relationship is not love, it is only the need for love. The kind of intimacy based on need in a one-sided relation is not true self-disclosure. It is merely vulnerability without virtue.

Jessica sought counseling when the latest in a series of relationships with men ended with her feeling humiliated and hurt. Her story was a familiar one. Carl, who had recently been divorced, and with whom she had become involved sexually, told her that he wanted to move in with her so that they could begin to plan their marriage. His view was that they needed to establish a real basis of love before making a decision to marry. She agreed, only because she felt deeply in love with him and was afraid that by resisting this move he would end the relationship. She realized that allowing him to share the most intimate and personal aspects of her life made her vulnerable but considered that to be one way of showing her love.

It lasted only six months. During that time he ran up excessive charges on her credit card without her knowledge and became abusive when she tried to establish some ground rules for their domestic life. She came home one day to find him gone; he had left a note saying that he was tired of her nagging and complaining but no number for her to contact him.

"In a sense I was lucky," Jessica told her counselor. "It could have been worse. He was becoming violent and I was afraid that he might really hurt me. But I have really been damaged by this and am afraid that I can never really trust any man again. Why am I so foolish when it comes to love?"

Jessica has probably already bought the book *Women Who Love Too Much.* She will identify strongly with the suggestion that her problem was in loving too much and becoming too vulnerable and finally becoming a victim. Is she right? Is the danger in loving too much or in using vulnerability and self-disclosure as a way of being loved?

I think it is the latter. Jessica's need, like so many of us, was not to find someone to love, but to find someone to love her. The need for love can be the hidden drive in our feelings of love. Because love is based on self-disclosure, we are misled into thinking that love can be gained through self-disclosure and that loving with the hope of being loved in return is the key to intimacy.

Wrong! As Jessica discovered, vulnerability without mutual commitment and self-disclosure makes a mockery of intimacy. Her vulnerability and self-disclosure, without self-disclosure and commitment on Carl's part, was not wise and had no virtue. She had feelings of shame about the relationship from the beginning and ended up feeling humiliated and hurt.

It is not enough to know another person's name before entering a personal relationship, as my grandson has yet to learn. Being vulnerable without becoming a victim is a delicate balance between trust and caution. Loving freely without loving foolishly requires wisdom and spiritual insight. Knowing whom to trust and when to self-disclose is the key that opens the door to love. Knowing when to use the key is the wisdom of love.

The Key of Wisdom Is Loving Freely

If love were not freely given, it would not be love. When we place conditions upon our love, we are using love to control and manipulate others. At the same time, love is the giving of something precious and holy because it is the gift of ourselves to another. The wisdom in loving freely is being free not to give of ourselves when that gift will not be respected and valued. Jesus minced no words when he warned against indiscriminate love. "Do not give what is holy to dogs; and do not throw your pearls before swine, or they will trample them under foot and turn and maul you" (Matt. 7:6).

How can we set criteria for whom and when we love without setting conditions upon our love? The answer is quite simple. When I set conditions on love I say, in effect, "I will love you *if* you do what I want." This kind of love takes control of the other. Carl, who coerced Jessica into letting him move in with her, placed conditions on his love. He threatened to withdraw his love unless she gave in to his demand. He ended up controlling her and abusing her. In seeking his love, Jessica attempted to love freely but ended up loving foolishly. She failed to use the key of wisdom and set criteria for the giving of her love.

When I set criteria for love, I am saying, in effect, "I love you *because* you respect and value the dignity and integrity of my spirit." Love is the meeting and interchange of spirit through mutual self-disclosure and vulnerability. The key is the word *mutual*. When loving freely is mutual and when the value of the spirit of each is cherished and honored, love is faithful, fruitful, and wise.

• It is the wisdom of love to disclose one's intention in the offer of love. Motives are not the same as intentions. I may not always know my own motives and may have no clue as to the real motives of others. An intention, however, reflects a purpose I can be expected to disclose and for which I can be held accountable.

In all human relationships, what we intend by our words and actions is what we are held morally responsible for. When I sign a contract to purchase a car, my intention to make payments is captured by the terms of the contract supported by my signature. If my motive is really to defraud the bank that loaned me the money to buy the car and not make the payments, the bank retains the title to the car. The bank may appear to make loans freely—but never foolishly! They have certain criteria by which they determine to whom they will make the loan, and they set clear conditions.

Love cannot set conditions, otherwise it would not be love. But love does set criteria. Among these criteria is that of intentionality. In this case, the disclosure of one's intention is keyed to the value and freedom of the other. We discern the intentions of others by measuring their words and actions against the value we place on ourselves. While intentions may not be disclosed formally as vows (this is the purpose of a marriage ceremony), they are always present in relationships involving friendship and love.

Quite clearly, Carl did not disclose his real intentions toward Jessica when he did not respect her freedom and dignity as a person. Blinded by her own need to control him through the giving of her own love, she failed to perceive his real intention toward her and became the victim of her own vulnerability. If the value of her self as a person had been at the forefront, rather than her need to be loved, she would have quickly discovered his unwillingness or incapability to affirm and support the freedom and dignity of her own spirit.

- It is the wisdom of love to preserve the freedom of the other as the object of love. Anne Morrow Lindbergh touched the core of this wisdom when she wrote: "Him that I love I wish to be free—even from me."[1] Only when one relinquishes all claim on the other—and this is the paradox of love—only then can one possess the other. Until the other is freed by us not to love, only then can we trust the wisdom of love.

Loving freely does not mean giving way to one's own need for love, nor does it mean giving oneself away to the other. But when love does not promote the freedom of the object of love, it becomes compulsive and coercive. Neither Jessica nor Carl were free in their love. Each sought to control the other, Carl through withholding love until he got his way, and Jessica through giving love in order to bind him to her.

The black humor of the bumper sticker is a blatant reminder of how near to the surface raw violence can lie when the compulsion to control takes the form of love. "If you love something, set it free. And if it doesn't come back, hunt it down and kill it."

The loss of freedom in a relationship driven by emotional need does not come with advance warning. Unlike a road sign that reads "Danger! Oncoming Traffic," it is more subtle and more subliminal. In a relationship of emotional codependency, the loss of freedom is like the proverbial frog in a kettle where the water is gradually warmed until the frog begins to cook. Adjustment to the rising temperature preserves the feeling of normalcy until it is too late.

• It is the wisdom of love to set boundaries that define one's own spiritual and personal integrity. Where these are lacking, one is vulnerable to the need to be loved as the primary value for the self. In this case, whoever is willing to provide that need becomes the boundary for the self. The violation thus occurs at the very outset, and the violence is not far in the future.

If one lacks these internal markers of spiritual and personal integrity, the answer is to seek the wisdom that comes "from above," as James suggests. This wisdom is "peaceable, gentle, willing to yield, full of mercy and good fruits" (3:17). This is spiritual wisdom and can be found where the Spirit of God is present in the lives of those who manifest the fruit of the Spirit.

• It is the wisdom of love to care for one's spirit in the mutual gift of love. When love issues from the human spirit, it carries with it the mystery and uniqueness of the self. This is the assumption behind Paul's statement: "What human being knows what is truly human except the human spirit that is within?" (1 Cor. 2:11). Except we give of our spirit to another, we cannot give love; for love is more than a caress and intimacy more than proximity.

The human spirit is the core of the self as desiring, cherishing, longing, and believing. As we grow and develop as persons, our spirit selects and assimilates from all of our experiences; it creates and colors life with the tension and texture that vibrate with urgency and repose in peace. The spirit wills and resists, opens and closes, gives and receives.

To share our spirit is to receive the other into the sacred shrine of what is most personal and dear; to share the spirit of the other is to be welcomed freely and trustingly into their holy of holies. Wisdom is spiritual insight into what is most precious in human life. Wisdom is the care with which we guard the entrance to our own spirit and the candor with which we seek admittance to the spirit of another.

Carl and Jessica shared emotional, physical, and domestic intimacy, but their relationship was lacking in spiritual care. While they may have each thrown a few pearls into the mix, these were quickly trampled and they each turned away feeling abused and wounded. Love without mutual care of the spirit is spiritual abuse and finally is revealed not to be love at all.

The virtue of wisdom is admired by all of us, especially when we have loved foolishly. The answer is not to renounce love in order to avoid being hurt but to seek the wisdom of love in order to be healed. This is the wisdom that comes from above. It is spiritual wisdom, and it produces spiritual maturity, spiritual balance. If it is our intention to receive it, we should know that it is God's intention to give it. His love is free and faithful.

8

Honesty

Being Truthful without Shaming Others

But speaking the truth in love, we must grow up in every way
into him who is the head, into Christ.

Ephesians 4:15

"The simple truth is harder to tell than a lie," complained one of the characters in a play by Christopher Fry. The boy's father had died, and the villagers came out to where he was caring for his father's sheep to tell him. He does not want to hear this tragic fact and denies that it is true.

The news did not escape him, of course. It lodged in the core of his brain like a speck of sand in the corner of his eye. The truth of his father's life, however, was like the blue sky across which the warm sun slowly moved on its predictable path. One does not easily exchange this kind of truth for a chilling fact. He stood blinking, hoping that he could dislodge the sharp pain before he began to cry.

What is factually true can be dreadful and shattering to the personal truth that binds our fragile lives to the intangible realities of life and love. Facts, not fantasy, are what sometimes drive us to the point of insanity. Compulsive preoccupation with proving and testing every fact in life may be a sign of mental illness, not of moral honesty.

"Always tell the truth," we are told from our earliest years. But the truth is sometimes painful to ourselves and often destructive to others as the following dialogue demonstrates.

"I saw you sitting in the park today with a strange woman."

"She was not a strange woman but one of the secretaries who works in our office."

"Oh, so you know her quite well, I gather. She appeared to be interested in you."

"We were talking. She was telling me about the problem she has been having finding an apartment. In fact, she said that she had been sleeping in the park the last few nights. I expressed concern. It was all quite innocent."

"Do you expect me to believe that? I am your wife. You haven't had a real conversation with me in months and then I find you sharing the intimate details of the life of a streetwalker!"

"She's not a streetwalker. She simply has had a run of bad luck and ended up without a place to live."

"Oh, pardon me! You obviously think more of her than you do of me. You are probably having an affair with her, otherwise you would not be so quick to defend her virtue."

"I am not having an affair with her."

"But you enjoy her company, don't you? You have even thought of sleeping with her, isn't that true?"

"It's true—but it's not the truth."

"The truth," he said to himself, as the conversation abruptly ended, "is that our lives are a tangled web of pretense and distrust where truthfulness for the sake of simple honesty is more of a threat than a premeditated lie. Without the moral value of honesty, a relationship can only survive through some mutually agreed upon deception."

The Moral Content of Truth

"Do you swear to tell the truth, the whole truth, and nothing but the truth?" This is a familiar form of an oath when one takes the witness stand in a court of law. When an attorney insists on a yes or no, the witness squirms. Being forced to affirm a simple fact often yields a misleading conclusion with regard to the whole truth. Consider the case of Mr. Jones.

"Your car in fact went through the intersection when the light was red, did it not, Mr. Jones?" the prosecutor asks. As an explanation is not permitted, Mr. Jones is forced to admit that this was true. "Thank you, your honor, no further questions!"

Mr. Jones can only hope that he has an attorney skillful enough to elicit further information about the incident revealing that he was rushing his pregnant wife to the hospital and, as there was no traffic in sight, he drove through the red light in order to arrive before the baby was born. Rendering a verdict in this case requires a decision as to which of the "facts" carries the greater moral weight of law, an emergency involving human life or the letter of the highway traffic code.

The moral dimension of truth at the legal level presumes the virtue of honesty, both on the part of those whose sworn duty is to uphold the law and those who seek an exception from its penalty. If it can be shown that the traffic officer who wrote the citation has a history of falsifying information on his reports in order to gain a high rate of convictions, his pattern of dishonesty will undermine the credibility of his testimony in court. The "truth" of the written citation rests on the honesty of the person who wrote it.

If the prosecuting attorney can show that Mr. Jones's wife, though pregnant, was not really about to give birth and they were not rushing to the hospital, then Jones's testimony is not only untrue but his attempt to deceive the court and evade a penalty for a traffic violation shows him to be dishonest. The presumption of the honesty of those who testify to facts in a court of law is the moral basis of law.

At the personal level, the moral demands of truth-telling may require us to deny certain facts that are true in order to preserve a grasp on the whole truth. What is true should not be told if it will falsify our understanding of the truth. We can throw facts around as though they were bits of truth. But in fact, we have only "told the truth" to someone when what we tell enables them to grasp that reality we know to be "the truth."

Can the Truth Always Be Told?

"Am I going to die?" a patient queried her doctor.

The doctor pondered the question for a moment. He knew that such a question is not always a request for information; it may be a plea for a word of assurance to staunch the hemorrhage of fear. All the medical facts pointed to a diagnosis of terminal illness; his patient had only a few weeks to live at best.

"I honestly don't know," replied the doctor. "There are many factors outside of our control. Let's take it one day at a time."

The doctor was honest in admitting his unwillingness to give a final verdict. Yet, he did not tell the truth, for one cannot honestly face life without finally facing the truth of one's death. Uncertain as to how to give her accurate information that she could integrate into the truth of her own being, he sidestepped the issue. He wisely recognized the danger of destroying what hope she had, for hope is itself a positive value in fighting for one's life. Yet, he knew in his heart, he had not helped her integrate the fact of her imminent death into the truth of her life, a fact which, he presumed, she had already guessed. No one at medical school had prepared him for this task!

Truth includes a moral context as well as a factual probability. The moral context of truth is trust, for trust is the lifeline that keeps the vulnerable self from skidding on the glare ice of fact into the chasm of hopeless fear. Truth must be "held in trust" in order that the lifeline that connects us to hope may be preserved and strengthened. The deeper truth of life is the will to live and love; where that can be preserved and strengthened, the facts can be faced, even of one's own death. We need to know all the facts that we can bear in living truthfully as well as hopefully.

"How did I really do? Tell me the truth," insisted a student after giving her first talk before the class. The teacher is experienced and has an expert opinion and critical objectivity by which to make an accurate assessment. Measured by the teacher's criteria, the student's presentation was amateurish and awkward. The problem is, what is the truth that the student really wants to hear? A wise teacher will say, "I am very proud of you for having the courage to get up there when I know that you must have been afraid. Tomorrow we will talk about some of the ways you can do even better."

Has the teacher been truthful? Not in a technical sense. But she has been honest in her concern for the fragile thread of self-esteem that the student has risked in the venture, and she has honestly pointed the student to a process for improving on her performance. To point out failure in the name of truth may be to write an insult on the face of hope.

In the comic strip "Peanuts," Lucy berated Charlie Brown scornfully. "You are an utter failure, Charlie Brown;

it's clear to everyone. It's written all over your face!" Charlie turned away dejected and said to Snoopy, "Just look at my face; don't write on it."

We must speak "the truth in love," wrote the apostle Paul (Eph. 4:15). There may be occasions when love demands that we be silent when telling the truth will only cause harm to those who trust us. Sometimes telling the truth can shame and hurt the very ones with whom we live. To betray a confidence by "telling the truth" may itself be a form of dishonesty, for honesty is bound up as much with trust as with truth.

Children have been known to blurt out facts about family matters that are true but are inappropriate. When we scold them for their careless talk, it is often because of our embarrassment and feelings of shame. In our eyes, the fact that what they said was true does not excuse them. They have not yet learned the moral lesson that truth can betray, harm, and even kill. Until children can be trusted to know the truth, they cannot always be told the truth.

Are we responsible always to tell the truth regardless of consequences?

"Is it not true that your father has been in prison?" a teacher asked his student in front of the class. "No, it is not true," responded the student, and so denied what was a known fact.

The boy was caught in a moral dilemma not of his own making. True, his father had a prison record, a fact that caused much distress and disgrace to the family. But the man was also his father, a truth that could not be denied and that the boy was willing to defend, even if forced to lie. The boy felt the exposure of the family secret before the class shameful, both to himself and to his father. Not willing to be shamed, the boy denied what was true for the sake of preserving his family's dignity.

The teacher asked an "untruthful question" by forcing the boy to reveal a fact that violated the deeper truth by which he lived every day of his life. For the boy to tell the truth in that situation would have caused his father shame. Indeed, by forcing the boy to expose the family secret, the teacher was shaming the boy as well.

In the end, we are compelled to admire the boy as having more virtue than the teacher. He has the virtue of loyalty, which is close to honesty. The boy, honestly, was simply not free to tell the truth! As he matures, he will discover other alternatives to lying when placed in such situations, though he may not honestly always be able to tell the truth.

When Telling the Truth Is Painfully Necessary

There are times when telling the truth is the only way to break a cycle of abuse within a family or relationship. Where the violation of another's personal being is kept secret for the sake of keeping the relationship intact and protecting the perpetrator, the truth must be told to those who can make an intervention and stop the abuse. In the case of chronic chemical or alcohol dependency, domestic violence, or sexual abuse, a family structure is dishonest when the secret is kept and the truth concealed.

When we look at the virtue of honesty as the moral context of truth, it becomes clear that "telling the truth" is far from an abstract moral principle. It is morally wrong to use the truth to shore up one's own moral status when it also shames and hurts others. One is simply not free to tell the truth in all situations. There are personal and family "secrets" that honestly ought to be kept.

But the moral context of truth-telling cuts both ways. When suppression of the truth perpetuates a moral wrong, as in the case of domestic or sexual abuse, the injured person needs the truth to be revealed as the first step toward freedom and healing. How the secret of abuse is exposed and what supportive structures are in place when this is done is a matter of tactics and strategy. Even here, simply "telling the truth" can cause further violence. The necessity for telling the truth nonetheless remains.

"Speaking the truth in love" means that truth must serve the moral value of love. Failure to speak the truth and expose the secret of abuse is itself a moral failure of love. The victim has only the truth as the first step toward freedom. "The truth will make you free," said Jesus (John 8:32). As the one who came as the very incarnation of truth, Jesus exposed the untruth of corruption, bondage, and dehumanizing relationships wherever he found them.

Truth seeks moral health and spiritual openness. Where there is spiritual bondage and abuse, truth must be revealed. Spiritual balance includes the virtue of honesty as the moral content of truth.

Honesty is a virtue because it is a sign of health and wholeness. We admire those who have this virtue and rely on them to preserve our peace and promote our personal well-being.

The Virtue of Honesty

When we admire persons for their honesty, we attribute to them the moral quality of being trustworthy and truthful in their dealings with us as well as with others. Honesty is a virtue because it demonstrates a consistency of character upon which we rely when we trust another's words and actions. Honesty does not stand or fall with each transaction in life but is bound up with the personal history of each person in relation to others.

Dietrich Bonhoeffer, who left the security of his office as a German pastor to enter the conspiracy against Hitler, once said, "What is worse than doing evil is being evil. It is worse for a liar to tell the truth than of a lover of truth to lie."[1] He was speaking of honesty as a virtue when he wrote that. The lover of truth is basically an honest person who has demonstrated a consistent pattern of truthfulness in word and deed. The liar is basically a dishonest person who will use the truth to deceive and manipulate others.

When evil appears in the form of truth, we are blinded to its moral danger because we ordinarily assume that behind true words is an honest person. This is why it is worse for a liar to tell the truth. The liar counts on our commitment to take a person at his or her word until proven otherwise. By that time, it is too late. The liar has deceived us by telling the truth and gaining this advantage over us.

When an honest person, for one reason or another, is caught in a lie, we immediately note the contradiction because we know the person to be basically honest in word and deed. When the person acknowledges the lie and seeks forgiveness, the virtue of honesty remains intact despite the lapse. If deception becomes a pattern and the telling of lies flagrant, then we would finally revise our judgment of the person's character because the virtue of honesty no longer is evident.

On the other hand, as Bonhoeffer suggested, if an evil person deceives us by using truth as a tactic for gaining our trust so as to do us harm, the act of deception reveals a basically dishonest person. We are more vulnerable when evil is disguised as truth because in that instance there is no virtue of honesty to which we can appeal, nor can we look for repentance to recompense the wrong we have experienced.

How do we recognize the virtue of honesty in others and how can we acquire it in our own lives?

Honesty Is a Moral Contract That Binds Word to Deed

The psalmist admires the virtue of those "who stand by their oath even to their hurt" (Ps. 15:4). Having made a commitment or promise, an honest person fulfills it even when it is inconvenient or costly.

"I will pay you $5 per acre cash rent," my father once promised the owner of the land on which he wished to plant a crop. The agreement stipulated that the one who paid the cash rent was entitled to the entire harvest regardless of how it turned out. With a good crop, my father could have far more income from the land than by paying the owner a share of the grain harvested, which was a normal arrangement when the owner shared the risk with the farmer.

In agreeing to a cash rent, the owner of the land settled for a guaranteed payment rather than a share of the crop and so avoided any risk. As it turned out, a hailstorm destroyed the entire crop shortly before it was to be harvested. My father not only received nothing back for his investment of seed and labor, but he still owed the cash rent. Where some would have pleaded hardship and expected the owner to forgive all or a portion of the cash rent, my father "stood by his promise even to his own hurt." It took several years to make good on what was owed. But, in the end, my father was known in the community as an honest man.

At some point, any commitment we make and promise we give may demand more of us than we realized at the time. Honesty is not paying our bills when we have the money, it is owning up to our obligations when doing so requires sacrifice and costly effort. There are always excuses for not fulfilling an obligation. But to use them is dishonest, for it breaks the moral contract between word and deed.

We become known as persons who possess the virtue of honesty when we stop blaming bad luck, unexpected circumstances, or other people when it comes time to fulfill an obligation, no matter how small or insignificant it may seem to us.

"I will pick up the kids after school today and take them to soccer practice," a mother tells her car-pool partner. But later in the day, she discovers that this is the same day that she invited her husband's boss and his wife over for dinner.

She has a good excuse for calling and backing out of the agreement to pick up the kids; it would not be dishonest to change the arrangement since she made the commitment without realizing that it was the same day as the dinner.

But honesty can be demonstrated by keeping the commitment and suffering the inconvenience and extra work for the dinner if it is within her capability. If it is not, of course, she simply will have to seek to make other arrangements. If she follows through with her promise, however, she will be known as a person who keeps her word. Honesty is not always the opposite of dishonesty—in this case, it would not be dishonest to admit that she forgot and ask to be excused. Honesty is the moral contract between word and deed, even when there are valid reasons to get out of the contract.

The virtue of honesty is achieved by habitual and regular fulfillment of what we have promised in the daily routine of life. We can be trusted to be truthful when the stakes are higher because we have consistently demonstrated honesty in the routine of daily life. Honesty takes practice, and practice begins when we wake up in the morning!

Honesty Is a Moral Legacy We Inherit from Others

"I know your father well," the banker told me when I went in to ask for my first loan to begin my own venture in farming. "If you are his son your signature is all the collateral I need to make this loan."

It was then that I discovered the moral legacy of honesty I inherited from my father. I did not have to "start from scratch," as it were, to build a foundation of honesty. His honesty was a legacy that could only be preserved by using it! It was mine to lose! And I suddenly realized the responsibility that came with this legacy.

Honesty is related more to character than to personality traits. And character is formed through the social structures in which self-identity is determined. We never start from scratch in life but emerge either with a substantial deposit or a significant deficit of character. Those who have no legacy of honesty enter life with two strikes against them, and some with three.

Some discover that they have "struck out" without ever having come up to bat! It is unfair in many cases, to be sure, but honesty is rooted in character. Until the virtue of honesty as a structure of one's character is known, words alone do not have the ring of truthfulness.

"I've applied for seven jobs the past three weeks," a friend confided to me. "I was told in each case that I could not be hired because I had no record of employment that indicated the necessary experience. How does one begin to gain experience when experience is a prerequisite?"

Good question!

The same could be said for honesty. If honesty is a prerequisite for being trusted as truthful, how can one achieve honesty without a legacy of honesty on which to build?

The days are long gone when one can go to the village banker and be recognized as an adult son or daughter of a family whose character is known and respected. This is true at least for most of us who live in urban and suburban areas. Unfortunately, the days are also disappearing when most young people enter into adult life having their self-identity formed through a strong family and community of character. When the moral contracts between word and deed are treated as inconvenient and dispensable, the moral legacy left is superficial and slippery. In this case the common wisdom is, "Slide out of it if you can. Cut your losses and find a new partner or different job as fast as possible."

If we feel cheated out of the moral legacy of honesty, we can begin to build one for the next generation. It only takes one generation to create a legacy. Several generations of moral bankruptcy can be turned around in one generation if the moral contract between word and deed begins to be practiced in everyday life.

Each family unit, however it is defined, is the moral equivalent of the "village" of yesteryear. For the next generation to emerge as the "son or daughter of" people who demonstrate the virtue of honesty requires that this virtue be achieved by the present generation.

The payoff for honesty is in the legacy it leaves, not the immediate benefits it gives. Perhaps we should add a paragraph to our last will and testament describing the moral legacy of honesty we intend to leave those who succeed us.

Honesty Is the Moral Fiber of Spiritual Fitness

Spirituality without honesty can be deadly! Take the case of Ananias and Sapphira, husband and wife who were caught in an act of deception that turned out to be fatal for both. In the early days of the first-century church, many people who owned land sold their property and gave it to the apostles for distribution to the poor. Those who demonstrated such extraordinary generosity obviously were admired by others.

Ananias and Sapphira, desiring to gain this favor among their peers, also sold their property. However, they agreed to keep back part of the proceeds for themselves and gave only a portion to the apostles. When this became known, Peter said, "Ananias, why has Satan filled your heart to lie to the Holy Spirit and to keep back part of the proceeds of the land? While it remained unsold, did it not remain your own? And after it was sold, were not the proceeds at your disposal? How is it that you have contrived this deed in your heart? You did not lie to us but to God!" (Acts 5:3–4).

When Ananias heard this, he fell down and died. His wife, Sapphira, appeared with the same story, and she likewise was struck dead.

The telling point in the story is that they lied and attempted to deceive the church (and God!) by pretending that they had given the entire amount. As Peter made clear, they were not obliged to give all or even any of the proceeds. It was their basic dishonesty that brought such dreadful consequences. Spirituality without honesty can be deadly!

Dishonesty and deception are forms of theft. One steals goodwill and honor from others by deceiving them. Paul's moral admonition is couched in practical terms. "Putting away falsehood, let all of us speak the truth to our neighbors, for we are members of one another. . . . Thieves must give up stealing; rather let them labor and work honestly with their own hands, so as to have something to share with the needy" (Eph. 4:25, 28).

Working honestly is the moral fiber of spiritual fitness and the spiritual force in truthfulness. The honesty in our work is measured by the motive and means hidden in the product itself. "To have something to share" is the goal of honest work. While one is not a thief, and thereby dishonest, in keeping something one has earned for oneself, a certain dimension of honesty is achieved by sharing the product of one's labor with those who have need.

Spirituality is not fundamentally an individual religious value; but rather, it is tested and played out in community. "We are members of one another," argues Paul. The fruit of the Spirit is displayed in those qualities that contribute to the character and quality of life in our primary social relationships.

The spiritual dimension of honesty goes beyond the moral law that forbids deception. While one can be a moral person by not stealing from another, one cannot be a spiritual person without sharing with another. It is that simple.

When we move beyond telling the truth to sharing the truth, we approach the altar of honesty on which we lay down our life and from which we receive the Spirit's gifts.

9

Tolerance

Being Agreeable without Agreeing with Everything

If it is possible, so far as it depends on you, live peaceably with all.

Romans 12:18

Some version of this letter has appeared occasionally in newspapers over the years.

Dear _____: My twenty-four-year-old son is coming to visit next month and wants to bring his live-in girlfriend with him. We are a traditional family and do not believe in living together before marriage. I told him that she was welcome to come with him but that they would have to sleep in separate rooms as long as they are in my house. He said that in that case, he did not feel free to come as this would offend his girlfriend. He says that I

108

am being intolerant. Don't I have a right to expect him to abide by our rules when he is in our house? (CONFUSED, in Centerville, Iowa)

The advice columnist's response is usually something along these lines:

Dear CONFUSED: While your son's values have changed, yours have not. Make it clear that she is welcome and will be treated with dignity and respect, but that they should also respect your position and accept the sleeping arrangement. They should also be tolerant of your values.

Because the question continues to emerge, my guess is that the advice, helpful as it is, has little practical effect. Tolerance is a virtue that is easier to admire than to practice. No one likes to be called intolerant. Yet, what some call tolerance others view as a slippery slope where convictions slide into compromise.

"George, I'm not going to invite the Wallaces over anymore. You and Jim get into such an argument over politics every time that it destroys the evening. Edith told me that Jim thinks you are the most intolerant person he knows."

"Me, intolerant! Do you know what that man thinks? He was out marching against the war in Vietnam while I was dodging bullets in the jungle, and now he thinks we should recognize their communist government. I can never accept his un-American views. How can one be tolerant of a person who holds those kinds of ideas?"

George resents being called intolerant. Everyone does. To call someone intolerant is to label them as bigoted, mean, and, well, let's say it—conservative! CONFUSED, in Centerville, Iowa, does not like to think she is intolerant. The values that once gave moral substance to her life are now viewed as a character defect by her "liberated" son.

She would like to have a peaceable relationship with her son and his friend. But in being agreeable to his demands she feels she would be compelled to agree with a lifestyle she views as morally wrong. Does tolerance mean that one has to agree with everything?

For George to agree with his friend Jim—that the United States had no right to impose a military solution on the political problems of Vietnam—and now agree to accept the communist government of that country is not tolerance. It is un-American! But Jim and Edith are not only friends; they are members of the same church that George and his wife attend. While George has not stated it openly, he has even questioned whether or not Jim could be a true Christian holding the views that he does. George also suspects that the pastor of the church holds views similar to Jim's. If that is true, it will not be long before he will have to leave and find another church more in line with his political convictions.

The Shame of Intolerance

No one likes to be called intolerant, and none of us likes intolerance in other people. What we don't like about intolerance is the shaming effect it has. The son's response to his mother's request that he and his girlfriend sleep in separate rooms when they were in her home was to charge her with being intolerant. His reply was not an objective judgment of her values but a response to what he felt was an accusation against the fact that they were living together without being married. To agree to her stipulation and sleep in separate rooms had the effect of shaming them for their lifestyle. In saying to his mother that this "would offend his girlfriend," he was speaking of his own sense of shame in a living arrangement of which his mother disapproved.

The mother, for her part, in speaking of her "traditional values" was also speaking out of her sense of shame at having her son and his girlfriend sleeping together in her house. The advice, "be tolerant of each other's values," does not work because it does not recognize the presence of shame that lies behind intolerance.

When we have deeply held convictions, whether they be moral values or ideological principles, they become part of our self-concept and personal identity. When these convictions are challenged either through verbal disputation or the behavior of others, our sense of self-worth is also threatened.

Intolerance is not just a dispute over differing values or ideas; it is a reaction of a self that feels threatened. Shame diminishes personal worth; not only are the values that we uphold challenged, but we feel unworthy as a person for holding these values.

As long as her son lives in another city, his live-in arrangement with his girlfriend is at a safe distance and the mother can maintain the integrity of her own life by concealing her son's lifestyle from her friends. She suffers from the shame of having a son who does not abide by her traditional values, but she has no way of imposing her values on him. Their relationship probably is one where his living arrangement with his girlfriend is never discussed openly. It is kept secret by tacit agreement for the sake of a mother/son relationship. There is no overt intolerance because, ordinarily, the situation does not present itself directly in her own home. The shame is there for both, but it is manageable.

The charge of intolerance emerges when a visit that includes the girlfriend is proposed. The discussion focuses on the difference in their values, but the shame each feels intrudes to the point of intolerance. The son cannot tolerate the sleeping arrangement proposed by the mother, as it increases the shame to an unbearable point. The mother cannot tolerate the idea of her son and his friend sleeping together in her home, as it brings her secret shame to the surface, and it is unbearable.

What we don't like about intolerance in others is the shame it produces in us. Having our ideas or values rejected can often feel like personal rejection, and we are left with a sense of unworthiness and shame. This makes the views of others intolerable to us, for we cannot give our consent and agreement to that which shames us.

A friend was dismissed from a high level executive position after a purported disagreement over philosophy and style of leadership. In talking with him, I asked, "How do you feel?" His reply was, "It is one thing to be told that someone does not like your work; it is another to be told that they don't like you."

What appeared to others to be a case of conflict and disagreement over leadership style was actually, at its core, a case of intolerance. When we are puzzled as to why people cannot find ways to work out disagreements, we fail to see that intolerance, with its shame-based core, is at work.

Tolerance cannot be practiced where shame is produced. The virtue of tolerance is that it upholds the value of other persons while discussing the values and ideas that they hold as personal convictions. In a context of confrontation, tolerance is needed even when agreement may not be possible. Tolerance is not the result of repressing disagreement and strongly held convictions, nor is it turning a blind eye toward ideas and actions that violate the integrity of persons and that threaten to compromise the truth of the gospel. There is a dimension of toughness that is part of true tolerance!

Tolerance with Toughness: A Biblical Case Study

When the apostle Paul wrote, "If it is possible, so far as it depends on you, live peaceably with all" (Rom. 12:18), he was careful to add, "if it is possible." Paul was a realist. He recognized that it is not always possible to live peaceably with everyone. "Welcome those who are weak in faith," he went on to say, "but not for the purpose of quarreling over opinions" (14:1). "Welcome one another, therefore, just as Christ has welcomed you, for the glory of God" (15:7).

Despite Paul's strong convictions, it is interesting that the charge laid against him by those who opposed his ministry was that he was too accommodating to those who did not measure up to the strict code of the Jewish law.

At the same time, Paul was firm with regard to excluding those who were perceived as destructive to the fellowship, and he did not hesitate to "name the names!" "Alexander the coppersmith did me great harm; the Lord will pay him back for his deeds. You also must beware of him, for he strongly opposed our message" (2 Tim. 4:14–15).

When the church at Corinth allowed a man to continue in fellowship who had committed sexual immorality of a kind not accepted among nonbelievers (a man living with his father's wife), Paul scolded them for their toleration of this person and urged them to exercise discipline by removing him from their midst for the sake of his spiritual healing and renewal (see 1 Cor. 5:1–5). In this case, their unwillingness to confront the man with his wrongdoing was not tolerance but collusion with sin.

Paul did not hesitate to confront even those close to him when he felt that they acted contrary to the truth. "But when Cephas came to Antioch, I opposed him to his face, because he stood self-condemned; for until certain people came from James, he used to eat with the Gentiles. But after they came, he drew back and kept himself separate for fear of the circumcision faction" (Gal. 2:11–12).

Nor should we forget the quarrel between Paul and Barnabas over the young man John Mark, who apparently withdrew from the first missionary journey due to some personal weakness. The contention between them was so severe that Paul and Barnabas separated, with Paul choosing Silas as his new partner and Barnabas departing in another direction with Mark (see Acts 15:36–40). There was no indication in Luke's account as to who was right or wrong. Barnabas probably leaned too much toward devotion and Paul toward discipline! There were boundaries to Paul's tolerance, which were tough on Mark and difficult for Barnabas. Perhaps this was why at first they made a good team. But the final test of tolerance is often reconciliation where estrangement has occurred.

Living and working together "peaceably" was not always possible, as Paul would be the first to admit. There was a certain toughness in his tolerance. It was tolerance that demanded loyalty to the common task and faithfulness to the gospel of Christ. Paul held Mark to his own high standards, whereas Barnabas argued for more latitude for failure on the part of the young man. In the end, however, Mark found a place beside Paul as evidenced by one of Paul's last letters to Timothy from prison. "Get Mark and bring him with you, for he is useful in my ministry" (2 Tim. 4:11).

If Paul at times appeared intolerant with the behavior of others, he was committed to tolerance as a spiritual virtue deriving from Christ himself. "Let each of you look not to your own interests, but to the interests of others. Let the same mind be in you that was in Christ Jesus" (Phil. 2:4–5). The virtue of tolerance is rooted in the spiritual grace of forgiveness, love, and affirmation of the value of others.

The Virtue of Tolerance

When we experience tolerance from another person, we feel accepted, included, and valued as a person. Jesus' tolerance toward those who were judged as unworthy was a scandal to the scruples of the self-righteous but a life-enhancing gift to those who experienced it. On one occasion when Jesus was dining at the home of a Pharisee, a woman of the street came in and washed his feet with her tears and dried them with her hair. The Pharisee said, "If this man were a prophet, he would have known who and what kind of woman this is who is touching him—that she is a sinner" (Luke 7:39). Jesus reminded the Pharisee that she had demonstrated the kind of welcome that he, as the host, had not performed, and then said to the woman: "Your sins are forgiven. . . . Your faith has saved you; go in peace" (7:48, 50).

In speaking of her sins he did not shame her, for he had already accepted and affirmed her value as a person. She experienced the virtue of tolerance from him while, at the same time, realizing that her own lifestyle was in need of repair and renewal.

When we respect others for their tolerance it is not because we view them as having no convictions. Rather, we perceive them as respecting our convictions even though we may not agree. One does not have to agree with everything another person thinks or does to express tolerance toward them.

Nor is tolerance a way of enduring something or someone for a time in order to get rid of them. There is a kind of "toleration" of others that is mixed with disdain. We might tolerate the undisciplined behavior of a friend's child while silently resenting the friend for not exercising more control. We tolerate a person who makes a fool of himself at a party or a discourteous sales clerk rather than make an issue of the incident. This kind of "toleration" is not a virtue, but sometimes it's a practical necessity!

When we experience true tolerance, we recognize it as a virtue and value this trait in others. We can achieve tolerance in ourselves by understanding and practicing three simple guidelines.

1. *The virtue of tolerance is respect for the convictions of others.* Convictions are usually expressed as opinions. Opinions are personal viewpoints on life offered to others as facts. An opinionated person is one who preempts the discussion with a viewpoint that shuts off further conversation. Whatever the subject, the opinionated person has an idea or a solution that is offered as the final word.

A high school senior offers her credo as a motto on the frame of her license plate: "My opinion is a gift—I give freely!" In person she adds, "I'm also opinion tolerant!"

We admire the person who has an opinion but is willing to listen to others. This is the beginning of tolerance. Behind some of our opinions are deeply held convictions. The opinionated person makes no distinction between a point of view (an opinion) and a conviction (a value). An opinion can be withdrawn or changed as long as it does not represent a conviction. Convictions lie closer to the core of a person's set of values and represent more of an investment of self-identity than opinions.

For example, in my opinion, parents are responsible for their children's behavior in public. The behavior of an ill-mannered child is a reflection on the parents, not the child. I freely express that opinion except when we are out in public with close friends whose children are acting up! To express my opinion at that point would be to shame the parents and be interpreted as intolerance. Intolerance has its roots in shame and is shaming in its effect. I must guard against mistaking my opinion for a conviction that demands defense and action. To insist that my opinion be heard and accepted in that context would make me an opinionated and intolerant person.

In another context, where the agenda is a discussion of how parents should discipline and teach children, I am more free to express my opinion, realizing that others may have different opinions and practices in this regard.

I have convictions regarding how children should be treated, however, that go beyond opinions. If a child is being abused, physically or emotionally, I must speak up on behalf of the child. Failure to do so would be to betray my conviction that each child is entitled to be valued and respected as a person. Toleration of abuse is quite different from toleration of bad manners, though both cause me concern. The question of how one should intervene in the case of known or observed abuse of a child or—for that matter—of another adult is one of strategy and tactics. The basis for taking action to report or intervene is a conviction, not merely an opinion, that one assumes others hold as well.

When we speak of tolerance, we are speaking of respect for the convictions of others that ordinarily do not demand action or intervention on our part. For example, in the case of George and Jim, cited earlier in this chapter, we have a case of deeply held convictions separating the two men, not merely opinions. Jim opposed the war in Vietnam out of personal conviction, while George defends his own participation in it with equal conviction.

If George wishes to achieve tolerance while holding to his own convictions, he might begin the conversation something like this: "Jim, it must have been hard to take a stand against the war at the time you did and be called unpatriotic and a communist sympathizer. You must have felt strongly about what you did."

"As a matter of fact I did, George, and maybe I am still defending myself in your eyes, because I am well aware of the fact that you risked your life by entering the war while I ducked the draft by staying in graduate school. Is it possible that we both did what we thought was right?"

The virtue of George's opening in this conversation is that he attempted to understand the depth of the conviction by which Jim acted, even though George thought it was the wrong thing to do. This freed Jim to acknowledge the feelings that he had, and that he now has, regarding his relationship with George. Without using the word, Jim has spoken of the shame he felt and might still feel in realizing that George had only contempt for what he did.

2. *The virtue of tolerance is openness to the feelings of others.* By getting below the level of the political, moral, and philosophical content of our convictions, we touch the feelings that underlie our convictions and actions. The feel-

ings that underlie another's convictions can always be respected, even though we might disagree with the conviction itself. Mutual respect for these feelings provides a basis for a fellowship that permits each to hold to his or her own convictions. Openness to the feelings of others is the virtue of tolerance.

The more difficult case is that of the mother and her son who is living with his girlfriend. The mother's convictions are grounded in what she considers moral and probably biblical reasons why living together without a marriage license is wrong. To accept this arrangement, even with regard to her son, would be to compromise this deeply held value and possibly even place her in conflict with her religious beliefs.

When the conflict is between two deeply held convictions, that of her commitment to her son and that of her sense of moral values, this mother faces a terrible dilemma. Now that the son wants to bring his girlfriend to visit, she is faced with a choice. In either case the alternative violates a conviction she holds dear.

In my earlier discussion of this case, I suggested that shame may well be the precipitating factor in the son's charge that the mother was intolerant. Shame is one of the deepest feelings a person can experience, because it diminishes one's sense of self-worth and value. Just knowing that her son is living with his girlfriend can produce shame in the mother, even though she is not guilty of any moral wrong herself. This is why shame is so different from guilt. One can feel shame without being guilty, because our sense of personal integrity is dependent to some degree upon those who belong to us.

The son may not feel guilty, because he has adopted a different moral reference point than his mother. He may no longer define morality in terms of a moral principle but by the quality of an actual relationship. He could argue that his relationship with his girlfriend is a moral one and that a marriage license granted by the civil law has no relevance to the moral quality of their relationship. He can argue this point with conviction! No doubt he has attempted to do so with his parents but has failed to persuade. The result is an uneasy silence—the unspoken disapproval of his parents, the cause of a deep sense of shame that his moral convictions cannot displace.

Are we at an impasse in this case? Does tolerance have its limits, and will the unresolved moral issues make it impossible for this family to embrace each other with love and affection?

I believe that openness to the feelings of others is a virtue and that it is an important ingredient in tolerance. Assuming this point, the mother might say something like this to her son:

"I have tried to put myself in the place of your friend, Jane, and I think that she must find it awkward and difficult knowing what our view of marriage is. And it must be hard for you, for I know that you love and care for me as much as you do for her. Your love for each other must be very solid to survive in such an unconventional way."

The power of this approach is in the magic words "it must be." This gives the person to whom one is speaking freedom to express the feelings that lie behind his or her convictions and actions. It is a verbal form of stepping into the shoes of another and affirming the reality and validity of that person's feelings. This is the key to respecting another's feelings. When we allow someone to express feelings, we validate those feelings and the person.

The feeling of shame is created when we are not validated at the level of our feelings. By saying, "It must be hard for you" and "your love for each other must be very solid," the mother affirms the feelings of the son and validates their mutual love, thus beginning to remove the shame that her silent disapproval has created.

The son might respond, "It has been hard, Mother, and it still is. I feel that I have failed you and Father, but my relationship with Jane is something I value very much. I know that must have been hard for you too, and I'm sorry to have caused you so much pain."

Real conversations do not always go according to script, we know, but the dynamics of this approach and response have been validated over and over again in real life. What the next scenario might be, for the son and his mother, is hard to predict. When mutual openness and respect for each other's feelings begin to emerge, however, there is hope that relationships can be healed and affirmed on the ground of mutual respect, and that tolerance will be expressed on both sides.

Tolerance does not erase the objective standards and criteria that determine our convictions but creates a pathway to the heart of each other through the labyrinth of failure and contradictions.

3. *The virtue of tolerance is allowance for the failings of others.* Intolerant people are often seen as judgmental, holding others accountable to their own moral standards. Jesus had something to say about this form of intolerance.

"Do not judge, so that you may not be judged. For with the judgment you make you will be judged, and the measure you give will be the measure you get. Why do you see the speck in your neighbor's eye, but do not notice the log in your own eye? Or how can you say to your neighbor, 'Let me take the speck out of your eye,' while the log is in your own eye? You hypocrite, first take the log out of your own eye, and then you will see clearly to take the speck out of your neighbor's eye" (Matt. 7:1–5).

In their own way, each of the disciples failed Jesus. They vied for positions of power when he had told them that those who serve have the highest honor. Peter was rebuked for attempting to dissuade Jesus from continuing on his path toward Jerusalem and, when put to the test at the final hour, denied that he even knew him! Judas, of course, betrayed him with a kiss. Yet, Jesus expressed tolerance toward them and made allowance for their weakness and failures.

"I have called you friends, because I have made known to you everything that I have heard from my Father. You did not choose me but I chose you" (John 15:15–16). He was aware of the fact that they would all fail him but gave them assurance that his peace and love would continue to be available for them.

"The hour is coming," Jesus told them, "indeed it has come, when you will be scattered, each one to his home, and you will leave me alone. Yet I am not alone because the Father is with me. I have said this to you so that in me you may have peace" (John 16:32–33).

Each of us has failed, most of all, our own standards. Very often we are the most intolerant with ourselves and so feed the shame that drives our intolerance toward others. We are our own harshest critics and the most unforgiving of our own failures.

A spirit of intolerance in a person is an indication of an inner battle between a sense of failure that produces shame and the setting of increasingly high standards in hopes of gaining self-worth. Intolerance toward others projects the failure outward upon them in the form of judging. Intolerance is thus a spiritual deficit and can only be overcome through the gift of grace and healing that "removes the log" in our own eye.

The virtue of tolerance is a mark of spiritual maturity, for it results from a healing touch from God's Spirit. "It must be hard for you," the Spirit of God whispers in our ear. "Come to me, all you that are weary and are carrying heavy burdens, and I will give you rest" (Matt. 11:28).

God's tolerance toward us is the gift of tolerance—the renewal of a broken spirit and healing of the shame that binds us.

10

Flexibility

Being Strong without Being Rigid

We who are strong ought to put up with the failings of the weak, and not to please ourselves.

Romans 15:1

It is not stress that causes a breakdown; it is rigidity. The capacity to flex under stress is a greater sign of strength than rigid resistance. This is as true for persons as for structures.

A visitor to the top of a skyscraper in Chicago was alarmed when he felt the building sway in the strong wind. "There is no need to worry," said a friend, who was also an engineer. "Deep underground the beams that hold this building upright sit on rollers so that the building can flex when buffeted by the wind. What you are experiencing is the sway that was built into the structure to keep it from breaking under the onslaught of a storm."

From a distance the building appears to be absolutely rigid, a towering mass of steel and concrete. Within the structure itself, one experiences the flexibility that gives it the strength to withstand the sudden movement of the earth during a quake as well as the fury of the wind at the top.

A building strong enough to withstand the force of violent shaking from either an earthquake or wind must also be flexible enough to yield to stress without breaking. This is also true of persons who demonstrate strength without being rigid. "Betty is one strong person. The death of her father, the accident that put her husband in the hospital, and the pressures of caring for three children under the age of seven would break the average person. I don't know where she gets her strength, but I would crack under the strain."

From the outside, Betty appears to be a tower of strength, rigidly resisting the tragic, unpredictable forces that have struck her like an evil east wind. Is she impassive and impenetrable, deflecting the pain and fear like a granite wall in a howling hurricane? Is she a stone mansion amidst the squatters' huts of life where most people live? Are some people just born with a spine made of steel?

I doubt it. She is not a marble monument impervious to her surroundings but a seaworthy sloop that is not afraid of deep water.

The Betty I know is strong not because she is rigid but because she is flexible. She sways and pitches on the stormy sea of her life like a ship whose sails have been shredded but whose hull flexes with every pounding wave without splitting a seam. The creaks and groans of her hidden timbers under stress would cause panic in the soul of one unfamiliar with a craft that bends but will not break. She keeps her bow headed into the wave, splitting its force and denying its will to swamp her deck with its crushing load.

No, her strength is not in the rigidity of steel but in the flexibility of spirit and flesh lashed together with the cords of faith. She takes hold of pain with passion and kneads it into unleavened bread to be saved for the Passover meal, a prelude to the journey toward the promised land. She turns anger into energy, driving the demons of doubt back into homeless exile, lighting every room in her dwelling with a candle of hope. She stirs God's rainbow of colors into the dark hues of sorrow that the random gestures of a fallen world have spilled into her life.

The measure of strength as a character virtue is not how much pressure one can exert against outside forces but how much stress one can absorb without breaking apart. The strong person is not impervious to pain but persevering in purpose.

Under stress in the garden of Gethsemane, Jesus called out in anguish with loud cries and tears, so much that his blood seeped through the pores of his skin (Luke 22:44; Heb. 5:7). At the same time, when the shadow of the cross crept into the inner sanctuary of his soul, convulsing him with fear, he found the strength to say: "Now my soul is troubled. And what should I say—'Father, save me from this hour'? No, it is for this reason that I have come to this hour" (John 12:27).

When we observe a person who demonstrates strength under pressure, we see the virtue of flexibility, a capacity to adjust to external forces without losing internal focus.

The Internal Dynamics of Flexibility

Metaphors help us identify the intangible aspects of the human spirit in its psychological and physiological operation. I have used the metaphors of a skyscraper and a ship to demonstrate the dynamics of flexibility and strength. Jesus was fond of metaphors, referring to himself as the vine and the disciples as branches (John 15). He spoke of himself as the good shepherd of the sheep and the door through which the sheep enter the sheepfold (John 10). He depicted wisdom as a man building a house on a foundation of solid rock rather than sand (Matt. 7).

I now use three metaphors to illustrate flexibility as a character virtue that persons who demonstrate strength under stress exhibit. The first is that of a gyroscope, the second a shock absorber, and the third a disconnect switch. Each points to an essential element of flexibility as a mark of spiritual fitness.

1. Keeping One's Balance: Flexibility as a Spiritual Gyroscope

The discovery of the physical phenomenon that a spinning object tends to remain in its original position despite pressures from the side is probably as old as the child's spinning top. The invention of the gyroscope by French physicist Jean Foucault in 1852 made what was an interesting scientific phenomenon into a practical device that is now found in steering devices (the gyrocompass) and stabilizing devices (the gyrostabilizer).

Today, almost every vessel of any size has a gyrostabilizer that serves to keep the ship level despite the motion of the waves. The huge spinning mass in the bowels of the ship offers strong resistance to the force of the waves that would cause it to sway from side to side during a storm or a rough sea. As the gyroscope leans with the ship under pressure, a counterforce in the spinning gyro tends to correct the sideways motion and returns the ship to an even keel. The gyroscope flexes with the movement of the ship, but its own strong inertia quickly pulls the ship back into its original position.

Keeping one's balance when exposed to the shock waves of misfortune, tragedy, or emotional pain requires an inner core of resistance. The person who demonstrates strength under these circumstances and is not "toppled over" has such an inner gyroscope that provides resistance. Flexibility rather than sheer rigidity permits the self to absorb the shock waves without breaking apart.

Once the gyroscope is attached to the ship at its center, it affects the entire ship. Similarly, the internal gyroscope of flexibility provides stability for the self in all directions and under all conditions. The psalmist expresses his confidence in this inner stability by the assurance that those who trust in God will never be moved: "I keep the LORD always before me; because he is at my right hand, I shall not be moved" (Ps. 16:8). "For the king trusts in the LORD, and through the steadfast love of the Most High he shall not be moved" (Ps. 21:7). "God is in the midst of the city; it shall not be moved; God will help it when the morning dawns" (Ps. 46:5). "Those who trust in the LORD are like Mount Zion, which cannot be moved, but abides forever" (Ps. 125:1).

It is not uncommon to read in the newspapers the testimony of a person who has experienced the shock of tragic loss and misfortune: "It is only my trust in God that keeps me going." Others respond in a similar way: "If I did not have the Lord as my refuge and strength, I could not continue to function."

Yet, many who say that they have strong faith in God during normal times fall into confusion and become disoriented during times of stress. The psalmist apparently is not referring to mere intellectual faith that breaks apart when buffeted by the storms of life. Rather, it is trust that provides balance and perspective under stress.

For some, faith is a static component in a rational belief system. Such faith is like a porcelain vase kept in a glass case for display. While it serves as an object of contemplation for the mind, it is highly vulnerable when shaken by emotional shock waves of doubt, grief, or fear.

The kind of trust that serves as a center of stability during times of stress is not static but has a movement of its own that resists the forces that attack from without. Trust is the movement of the spirit around the axis of love.

A child develops trust as the internal stabilizer of life. Trust grows by an interchange of spirit through openness to others. At first, the trust is weak because it is dependent upon the constant, familiar presence of those who provide care and attention. The spiritual core of the child is latent and untested. As the child sets in motion its own spiritual life through repeated responses to the spirit of others, an inner stabilizing force results so the child is able to keep its balance when experiencing brief separation from the caregiver. Trusting the object of love to return, the child develops an inner core of self-identity with respect to others.

Where the core of spirituality develops in a positive way, the child's gyroscope of trust is set in motion, keeping the self oriented to God, the source of its own goodness. Growing into adulthood, the spiritual core of trust internalizes its relationship with God's Spirit through the movement of prayer, worship, and reflection on the Word of God.

Trust, as I have indicated above, is the movement of spirit around the axis of love. The human spirit and human love provide the essential components of this inner "spiritual gyroscope." God's love and God's Spirit provide the energy and power that give the self an inexhaustible source of strength in the face of the stresses of life.

Lack of strength and failure of faith under stress is a spiritual deficit. Where there is no core of love as the axis for the movement of spirit, the human spirit itself is subject to erratic and unstable movement. "We must no longer be children," the apostle Paul wrote, "tossed to and fro and blown about by every wind of doctrine, . . . But speaking the truth in love, we must grow up in every way into him who is the head, into Christ" (Eph. 4:14–15).

Spiritual maturity—spiritual fitness—means having an inner gyroscope that keeps us in balance and gives us the flexibility to maintain trust in God while we make the critical adjustments required to weather every storm of life.

2. Maintaining a Level Ride: Flexibility as a Spiritual Shock Absorber

My first discovery of the value of a shock absorber occurred when, complaining of erratic steering, I took my car to a mechanic. The car seemed to dart all over the road when hitting even small bumps. I told the mechanic with some confidence that it was probably a problem of alignment, heeding my father's advice never to appear ignorant when taking a car for service.

Putting one hand on the front fender, the mechanic bounced the body of the car in a downward motion. When the car stopped its bouncing, he said, "You have worn shock absorbers. Your car is not supposed to bounce up and down like that. It affects the steering."

When the car was up on a hoist, the mechanic pointed out to me that the shock absorbers, elongated metal cylinders filled with oil, were leaking and inoperable. When he gave me the repair estimate for all four wheels, the shock revealed some problem with my own internal shock absorber!

Looking at a worn-out shock absorber removed from the car quickly revealed the secret of its operation. The part was actually composed of two metal cylinders, one slightly larger than the other, filled with oil. One end was attached to the wheel axle and the other to the body of the car. When a shock occurred, the cylinders compressed slowly due to the controlled transfer of oil within the cylinders. This prevented the shock from jolting the car. At the same time, the function of the oil in the sealed cylinder was to prevent a "bounce back" effect so that the car remained stable while the wheel moved up and down.

When advertisers wish to demonstrate the effectiveness of an automobile's ride, they sometimes place filled champagne glasses on the hood of the car and drive over a rough surface. To the observer, this demonstrates the car's smooth ride, a value that enhances the comfort level of the purchaser facing "sticker shock."

While all metaphors have their limits, the metaphor of a shock absorber seems particularly apt when we view life as a ride over a road filled with potholes, rocks, and other debris. The goal is to have a comfortable and level ride despite these obstacles.

We may view flexibility as the shock absorber of spiritual fitness. It produces a "level ride" with a minimum of "bounce back" when the car of life encounters the bumps and potholes that suddenly appear on our road. The apostle Paul had a marvelous way of putting it. "I know what it is to have little, and I know what it is to have plenty. In any and all circumstances I have learned the secret of being well-fed and of going hungry, of having plenty and of being in need. I can do all things through him who strengthens me" (Phil. 4:12–13). This sounds as if Paul had discovered how to have a level ride!

How did Paul reach this stage? "Through him who strengthens me," is his answer. Through the indwelling Spirit of Jesus, Paul has an internal shock absorber that levels out his life despite its ups and downs. Instead of dissipating his own strength through reacting to every twist and turn, he allows the Spirit of Jesus to cushion the shock.

Being flexible with regard to life's circumstances is also a way of preserving one's strength. Reacting to every obstacle and fighting every battle requires enormous emotional and spiritual energy. When every shock is felt as a direct jolt to our inner self, it reveals that we have no shock absorber. This constant bouncing around throws the whole of our life out of kilter.

Flexibility is a key ingredient in the spiritual maturity that enables us to absorb the bumps we meet when life develops a roller-coaster pattern. Jesus' creative flexibility can inspire us to imitate as best we can his unique ability to maintain a level ride in the face of repeated shocks from opposing forces. When some Pharisees came to warn him, "Get away from here, for Herod wants to kill you," he said to them, "Go and tell that fox for me, 'Listen, I am casting out demons and performing cures today and tomorrow, and on the third day I finish my work. Yet today, tomorrow, and the next day I must be on my way, because it is impossible for a prophet to be killed outside of Jerusalem'" (Luke 13:31–33).

The road to Jerusalem was rocky and rough, and the prospects for a safe arrival were not good. Yet Jesus absorbed these facts and kept a steady course. It is this same Jesus who rides with us and levels out the road.

3. Knowing When to Cut Loose: Flexibility as a Spiritual Disconnect Switch

I have a power chain saw that I use to cut large tree limbs. At the end of the chain blade closest to my hands is a large flat piece of metal with two positions. In the forward position the power to the blade is engaged. But if the chain throws a piece of the limb back toward my hand, it hits the plate and throws it back into the second position, which instantly cuts off the power to the blade. This is a built-in safety feature to prevent injury. Many power machines have such a switch to disengage the action of the machine from its power source.

One problem with rigid people is their inability to disconnect when engaged in some conflict or struggle. Like bulldogs that grasp an object in their jaws and refuse to let go even at the risk of dying, some persons lock on to an opponent or problem and lose their power to disengage.

Flexible people have a "disconnect switch" that releases them so they can disengage from a futile struggle that threatens to waste large amounts of energy and resources.

The virtue of flexibility gives wisdom for activating the disconnect switch when further effort becomes counter-productive, and even dangerous.

Luke records an incident that took place on Jesus' journey through the region of Samaria where Jews were not welcome, particularly when they were on a pilgrimage to Jerusalem. He sent messengers ahead of him hoping to find a village where they could stay and find refreshment and rest. But the reception was not cordial. "On their way they entered a village of the Samaritans to make ready for him; but they did not receive him, because his face was set toward Jerusalem. When his disciples James and John saw it, they said, 'Lord, do you want us to command fire to come down from heaven and consume them?' But he turned and rebuked them. Then they went on to another village" (Luke 9:52–56).

I fully understand the reaction of the disciples to this affront. Despite the fact that the Samaritans and Jews despised each other, it would have been hard not to take this rejection personally. To be refused entrance when hospitality was an almost sacred ritual for the Semitic people was a deliberate slap in the face, especially when the disciples were accompanying the long-awaited Messiah. Such provocation seemed to demand retaliation. They expected Jesus to provide them with the necessary ammunition. Instead, he activated the "disconnect switch," and they "went on to another village."

One of the marks of spiritual maturity is to possess the flexibility to "go on to another village"—to disengage from an encounter when the only point is to prove a point at all costs. This is easier said than done!

For example, when a divorce occurs, more often than not, one or both parties will continue to battle over issues related to the separation long after the final decree has been issued. The emotional need to retaliate in the face of perceived injustice or injury is powerful. The "disconnect switch" is difficult to activate when one continues to suffer devastating emotional pain.

Adult children sometimes carry with them long-standing grievances against parents who were abusive, neglectful, or dysfunctional in their own relationships. Failure to receive what was expected and needed at critical points in a relationship can cause parents to harbor grudges against their own children and siblings against each other.

Chronic emotional and spiritual fatigue due to the inability to throw the disconnect switch robs many people of joy and fulfillment in life. The decision to "go on to another village" illustrates the wisdom of discerning the proper point of disengagement from conflict and confrontation when no healing or reconciliation can take place.

At the same time, there are some whose disconnect switch is always on "ready alert." At the slightest provocation or discomfort in a relationship, they cut loose and cut off others. Flexibility as a mark of spiritual fitness includes a readiness to confront and resolve conflict through communication and negotiation. A tendency to break off communication and disconnect prematurely is a sign of rigidity rather than flexibility.

The spiritual dimension of the virtue of flexibility begins with the acceptance of one's own forgiveness and healing through God's Spirit. The affirmation of this acceptance is gained through fellowship with those who are spiritually balanced and steadfast in love.

Avoid the skyscraper types who seek to rise above others as a way of dominating the skyline. Seek out those who are seaworthy types, those whose hidden timbers creak and groan under stress, but who keep their bow headed into the waves and who, at the same time, keep their eyes open for capsized crafts in order to bring others aboard to safety.

11

Serenity

Being Calm
without Being Detached

And the peace of God, which surpasses all understanding, will
guard your hearts and your minds in Christ Jesus.

Philippians 4:7

Of all the attributes by which God has been depicted,
serenity was the favorite of the early Christian theologians.
They placed God beyond earthly passion and prejudice,
free of all desire and emotional turmoil. While humans
were torn by conflict and enraged by emotion, the divine
being was viewed as resting in perfect repose, his tem-
perament without passion and his love without lust.

In their minds, they could attain divine perfection only
through absolute detachment from human passion. The
fact that such a God was inaccessible, and finally irrele-
vant, did not deter some from attempting to emulate the

133

divine image through fantastic attempts to detach them-selves from earthly desires. Some withdrew into the bar-ren landscape of the desert in hopes of a new birth of spir-ituality. The hermits sought piety in isolation from people, the monks in rejection of passion.

That humans should long after a life of serenity is not surprising. Daily life is a cacophony of clamor and clutter. Unruly passion and unfulfilled desire are the invisible house dogs that nip at our heels during the day and howl at the moon in the night. What worry does not disturb, anxiety will not allow to rest. If lack of inward peace and outward calm is due to sin, then salvation is the search for nirvana—the virtue of absolute detachment.

Stir up these ingredients and you have the makings for an endless variety of human religions. If there is no god, one must be invented. If there is no peace on earth, heaven must be created. Serenity is a state of mind; evil does not exist. The "science of serenity" appeals to those whose belly is full but whose mind is vacant. Reverse that equa-tion and a different religion will emerge.

What shall we say to this? Is serenity possible only through detachment and denial? Is life calm only when the sea is silent and the wind holds its breath? Is serenity what some achieve as an altered state of mind through a chem-ical substance, while it remains an elusive dream for those whose only companion is the incessant cry of an infant, the roar of the factory floor, or the blare of electronic music? Is being alone the only refuge from too much togetherness? Why then is the pounding of the restless surf more calming to the soul than an empty house?

Serenity in the Midst of the Storm

The biblical profile of serenity is not that of a detached deity but of God in the midst of human life, fully exposed to tears, tragedy, and torment. Jesus said of himself that he was the very reality of God in a form that could be touched by human feelings and human hands (see John 14:1–14). The life of Jesus is a study of serenity, manifesting calmness without being detached.

Caught in a sudden storm on the Sea of Galilee, the disciples rowed furiously through the hours of the night. When their boat was in danger of being swamped by the waves, they awakened Jesus, who had been sleeping on a cushion in the stern. "'Teacher, do you not care that we are perishing?' He woke up and rebuked the wind, and said to the sea, 'Peace! Be still!' Then the wind ceased, and there was a dead calm. He said to them, 'Why are you afraid? Have you still no faith?' And they were filled with great awe and said to one another, 'Who then is this, that even the wind and the sea obey him?'" (Mark 4:38–41).

Admittedly, this was a dangerous situation and cause for panic. That Jesus could sleep during the howling wind and shouting of the men may have been due to his great fatigue but may also have been a sign of his inner calm. He was hardly a detached person, for his fate was bound up with the others in the boat. His attachment to them was the basis for their accusation that he did not care. Their fear rose to the stage of panic. And when panic strikes, no one can be permitted to be exempt!

For the disciples, the miraculous stilling of the wind and waves was a sign of Jesus' extraordinary power over the natural elements. His rebuke to them concerned the role of faith in controlling their own human spirits. Calmness does not mean the absence of fear but the management of fear by faith. Peace is not the absence of forces that are in conflict but holding together all of the pieces in order to achieve a harmony of wholeness, when everything seems to be breaking apart.

The Hebrew word for peace is *shalom*, which is understood to be a state of wholeness, reconciliation, and rest, not the absence of conflict. Serenity, thus, is the state of existing in *shalom* with full awareness of all the factors that determine the situation. For Jesus, the bond of his inner spirit with God as his Father was as much a factor in the situation as was the threat of the storm.

Near the end of his life, when the circumstances were far more threatening for him than the storm in the boat, Jesus told his disciples: "Peace I leave with you; my peace I give to you. I do not give to you as the world gives. Do not let your hearts be troubled, and do not let them be afraid" (John 14:27).

This kind of peace is best described as serenity in the midst of the storm. Remaining calm without being detached is a mark of spiritual fitness. The psychological state of fear, detached from the spiritual reality of faith, leads to panic and loss of control. Emotions without spiritual vision and guidance are like boats adrift in a stormy sea without rudder or compass. Serenity is the spiritual gift of peace amidst the confusion and conflicts of life.

The Spiritual Gift of Serenity

The human spirit is the integrating aspect of the self, bringing vision and clarity to the mind and the emotions. The spiritual life of the self is not a religious aspect added to the self, but it is the core of the self as created in the image and likeness of God.

Human life is "God-breathed" life. The Hebrew concept of the human self is depicted in the original creation account. "Then the LORD God formed man from the dust of the ground, and breathed into his nostrils the breath of life; and the man became a living being" (Gen. 2:7). The Hebrew word for "spirit" and "breath" is the same *(ruach)*. The breath of God is the Spirit of God.

The human spirit is an inverted loop of the divine Spirit. This thought is captured in the proverb: "The human spirit is the lamp of the LORD, searching every innermost part" (Prov. 20:27). Spiritual balance includes serenity as a spiritual gift available to each one of us through the exercise of spiritual perception, counsel, and healing.

Spiritual Perception: The Vision of Serenity

The feeling that life is unfair and that injustice has robbed one of what is rightly deserved is a familiar childhood trauma and, for some, a continuing complaint. Few things disturb our peace so much as a feeling of injustice. And nothing feeds our feeling of injustice as much as the prosperity and success of those who do not deserve it!

Rob came to my office livid with anger. "I have contributed more to the success of my company than any other employee. Fifteen years of faithful service, an unblemished work record, and a proven ability to bring in new business and increase profits—all disregarded when I lost the promotion to the boss's nephew!"

"But that's the prerogative of being a boss," I responded, hoping to disarm his rage.

"But it's not only unfair, it's a mockery. His nephew has only been with the firm for one year; he is a manipulator of others and basically incompetent. We have all had to cover up for him when he made mistakes. To give such a scoundrel this job and overlook my own performance is an outrage. I have suffered long enough with this kind of unfairness in our company, and this time I am going to confront it, regardless of the consequences."

As I listened, it became clear that this incident was only the latest in a series where Rob felt that he was being treated unfairly and that other people less deserving were getting what he felt belonged to him. His litany of injustices included members of his own family and, because he was a man of strong religious convictions, accusations against God for allowing these injustices to happen.

Ultimately, if we have any faith in God at all, we expect that he will reward us for what we have done that is good and punish those who are evil and do wrong. The human spirit is outraged when the righteous suffer and the unrighteous prosper. This is a familiar theme in the Bible.

Jesus dealt with it in his parable of the laborers in the vineyard. The owner hired workers early in the morning for a stipulated price for the day and sent them out. Later in the day, he found other workers and sent them out. Finally, near the end of the day, he found other workers who were idle and hired them also, telling them that he would pay them "whatever was right."

When it came time to pay wages to all of the workers, the owner gave those who had only worked one hour pay for a full day. Those who worked the whole day thought that they would thus receive more than the agreed price because they had worked longer. When they received only what had been agreed on, they were angry and grumbled against the owner. But the owner replied: "Friend, I am doing you no wrong; did you not agree with me for the usual daily wage? Take what belongs to you and go; I choose to give to this last the same as I give to you. Am I not allowed to do what I choose with what belongs to me? Or are you envious because I am generous?" (Matt. 20:13–15).

In the parable of the prodigal son, when the father welcomed back the younger son and gave him a party, the elder brother complained: "Listen! For all these years I have been working like a slave for you, and I have never disobeyed your command; yet you have never given me even a young goat so that I might celebrate with my friends. But when this son of yours came back, who has devoured your property with prostitutes, you killed the fatted calf for him!" (Luke 15:29–30). "It's not fair!" protested the elder brother. He perceived the forgiveness extended to his brother as a wrong done to him. Comparing his own situation with that of his brother created a feeling of injustice.

Fairness can be a matter of perception. When we compare what we receive in life with what others receive, we will usually find some injustice and someone to blame. One of the sources of chronic unrest and unhappiness is the feeling that life is not fair and that others have treated us unjustly.

In the Old Testament, the psalmist discloses a personal experience of this sort (see Ps. 73). He begins by asserting his perception of God: "Truly God is good to the upright, to those who are pure in heart" (73:1). This also entails the conviction that God will punish those who are not upright. As it turned out, he became angry and upset when he saw "the prosperity of the wicked. . . . For they have no pain; their bodies are sound and sleek. They are not in trouble as others are; they are not plagued like other people" (73:3–5).

"All in vain I have kept my heart clean and washed my hands in innocence," he complained. "For all day long I have been plagued, and am punished every morning" (73:13–14).

It is easy to see what has happened. His perception of God was one of perfect justice measured by how he fared as compared with those less worthy. His own well-being and sense of peace is now dependent upon the fairness with which God treats him as compared with others. Then he makes an insightful discovery and gains a new perception: "But when I thought how to understand this, it seemed to me a wearisome task, until I went into the sanctuary of God; then I perceived their end" (73:16–17).

The issue of God's justice is not determined by putting God on trial every day with regard to the advantage others gain over us. When we base our perception of fairness only on immediate gains or losses in life as compared with others, we are almost certainly going to be outraged. Each incident in which we are treated unfairly will disturb our peace and destroy our serenity.

The neighbor who farmed next to my father's farm had a field that lay on a sloping rise, entirely visible from our house.

My father had a rule never to work in the field on Sunday, a tradition taught and embodied in the religious ethic of the entire community. This neighbor was a nonchurchgoer, and he seemed to take pains to work in that particular field on Sundays. From spring to fall, every time that field needed work, he would be out with his tractor on Sunday.

My father appeared to pay no attention to this brazen act, but my mother was deeply offended. She fretted about it all summer, whenever the neighbor was working the field. Secretly, as it turned out, she expected a hailstorm or some other disaster to strike the man's crop as a sign of divine retribution. In the fall, instead, he harvested a bumper crop from the field—on Sunday of course!

When my mother finally exploded with frustration at the failure of divine intervention, my father simply said, "The Lord does not settle his accounts every October."

As I reflect on this incident, it seems to be exactly what the psalmist described as his own experience. His outrage at the injustice of the prosperity of the unrighteous as compared with his own misfortune caused such turmoil as to turn his soul toward bitterness and anger. Similarly, my mother allowed the neighbor's disregard for what she considered to be a divine law to cause her to live with growing resentment and a sense of injustice.

Serenity is something that we can achieve through the gift of spiritual perception. We gain this gift through listening to the wise counsel of the Spirit speaking to our spirit.

Spiritual Counsel: The Wisdom of Serenity

From time to time most of us talk to ourselves—if not audibly, then silently in our thoughts. "That was really stupid," I say to myself when I delete a file on the computer without a backup copy.

The psalmist, to whom I referred above, probably talked a lot to himself when he felt God was treating him badly.

He admits to being "stupid and ignorant" when his soul was so embittered. "When my soul was embittered, when I was pricked in heart, I was stupid and ignorant; I was like a brute beast toward you" (73:21–22). When he was thinking this way, he was giving himself bad counsel.

Serenity is not only the gift of spiritual perception, it is the practice of spiritual counsel. The psalmist has discovered this gift and is now ready to practice spiritual counsel: "Nevertheless I am continually with you; you hold my right hand. You guide me with your counsel, and afterward you will receive me with honor. Whom have I in heaven but you? And there is nothing on earth that I desire other than you. My flesh and my heart may fail, but God is the strength of my heart and my portion forever" (73:23–26).

Spiritual counsel is the beginning of wisdom and a step toward serenity. The psalmist again testifies to this fact: "The LORD is my chosen portion and my cup; you hold my lot. The boundary lines have fallen for me in pleasant places; I have a goodly heritage. I bless the LORD who gives me counsel; in the night also my heart instructs me. I keep the LORD always before me; because he is at my right hand, I shall not be moved. Therefore my heart is glad, and my soul rejoices; my body also rests secure. For you do not give me up to Sheol, or let your faithful one see the Pit" (Ps. 16:5–10).

"The LORD gives me counsel; in the night my heart instructs me." This sounds like the kind of self-talk most of us do at times. The Psalms are filled with exhortations given to one's own soul. "Why are you cast down, O my soul, and why are you disquieted within me? Hope in God; for I shall again praise him, my help and my God" (Ps. 42:5; see also 42:11; 43:5; 57:8; 103:1–2; 104:1; 116:7; 146:1).

Talking to our own soul by calling attention to the promises of God is what I mean by spiritual counsel. The heart is not only the source of feeling for the Hebrews, but it is the source of contemplation and meditation. When the psalmist says, "My heart instructs me," he is referring to the inner counsel of the human spirit under the tutelage of the Spirit of God. Spiritual counsel gives vision, clarity, hope, and healing to the self amidst conflict and confusion.

Serenity is not a feeling that comes by detaching oneself from inner conflicts and external threat. Nor does one achieve serenity by seeking to escape from the ordinary into a state of extraordinary peace. Serenity is spiritual perception that integrates the extraordinary into the ordinary. When a person brings the vision of a larger purpose and meaning to life into his or her concrete situation and experience, a new picture comes into focus. Serenity is spiritual counsel one receives into the soul as a deeper wisdom, such that a new capacity to grasp the whole of reality emerges. When spiritual perception and spiritual counsel do their work, spiritual healing results and the gift of serenity is received.

Spiritual Healing: The Gift of Serenity

The psalmist gives testimony to the healing power of serenity. "I keep the LORD always before me; because he is at my right hand, I shall not be moved. Therefore my heart is glad, and my soul rejoices; my body also rests secure" (Ps. 16:8–9).

We can view the heart as the center of feelings and thoughts, the soul as the core of the human spirit, and the body as the extension of the self as a physical being. In all three spheres we are subject to conflict, distortion, and injury. It is the heart that feels fear, thinks irrational thoughts, and experiences the pain of injustice. It is the soul as the core of the self that feels abandoned, lonely, and estranged from God and others. It is the body that suffers injury and deprivation, that becomes subject to disability, disease, and finally death. Serenity is lost when these components of the self are damaged or split off one from the other.

Spiritual healing is the integration of the heart, soul, and body into the core of spiritual life as having a destiny and purpose given to it by God. "I shall not be moved," asserts the psalmist who has received this spiritual healing. Serenity is the assurance that nothing can destroy the self or cause it to be lost when it is grasped by the power of God's love and grace.

"We know that all things work together for good for those who love God, who are called according to his purpose," asserted the apostle Paul (Rom. 8:28). Not all things are good, nor do bad things produce good. It is God who works good in spite of bad things that happen. Spiritual perception and spiritual counsel give a new perspective and meaning to life along with the power of faith to sing a new song of courage and hope. "For I am convinced that neither death, nor life, nor angels, nor rulers, nor things present, nor things to come, nor powers, nor height, nor depth, nor anything else in all creation, will be able to separate us from the love of God in Christ Jesus our Lord" (Rom. 8:38–39).

Serenity is being under control, rather than being in control or being controlled. Those who want to be in control of every situation soon go out of control through anxiety and stress. Being controlled by others and the relentless demands of duty and desire can result in spiritual defeat and suicidal despair. Those who are under the control of the Spirit of God enter into God's own peace and serenity, with the creative freedom to have faith and live with hope.

Serenity is an extraordinary calm in the midst of ordinary life; it is being at peace amidst conflict and confusion. Serenity is a mark of spiritual fitness, a gift that is available to each of us as the healing power of spiritual perception and spiritual counsel. It is a God-breathed gift that touches the core of our spiritual being.

12

Faith

Being Visionary without Going out of Focus

Now faith is the assurance of things hoped for, the conviction of things not seen.

Hebrews 11:1

The woman's face was a tormented image of despair and grief. Her two young children had died in the bombing of the federal building in Oklahoma City early in 1995. The camera captured the pathetic image of her silently weeping and clutching two teddy bears at the nationally televised memorial service.

Some weeks later, in response to a reporter's question as to how she managed to face life with hope and optimism following the loss, the woman replied, "It is my faith that keeps me going. Without faith in God I don't know how I could live through this loss and rebuild my life." Some months later, when this same woman had surgery allowing her to conceive again so that she might have other children, television reporters called it a "miracle of faith."

It was not the surgery but the woman's vision of having more children, reuniting with her estranged husband, and the beginning of a new life that evoked the response, "a miracle of faith." The medical marvel is a product of technology and science. The human spirit is not so easily remanufactured when it has been broken.

We cannot help but admire persons who survive difficult ordeals without collapsing into self-pity and bitterness. How does one achieve this kind of faith in the face of adversity and tragic loss? Is faith a spiritual gift to the chosen few, or is it a resource each one of us has at our disposal if only we can find the key?

It was a desperate father who first uttered the words, "I believe; help my unbelief!" When the disciples failed to heal his son, he turned to Jesus with a cautious request, "If you are able to do anything, have pity on us and help us."

"If you are able!—All things can be done for the one who believes," replied Jesus. The mild rebuke was coupled with a challenge and promise. Faith born of desperation may not be pure, but it is persistent.

"I believe; help my unbelief," was the father's tortured reply (Mark 9:22–24). As much as he loved his son and longed for his healing, could he really be sure that his faith did not have a fatal flaw of doubt? Could any of us be certain?

The boy was healed. As for the father, was his request granted because he had sufficient faith despite his disclaimer, or because his desperation overcame his doubt? Part of faith is knowing that it is not our faith but the one in whom we put our trust that turns the key. The test of faith is the capacity to believe when there are no visible evidences on which to rely. It is not the absence of evidences that evokes faith; it is just that some of the evidences on which faith rests are invisible, though real.

When the Clouds Eclipse Our Faith

"All things can be done for the one who believes!" Who of us would like to be put to such a test? However much faith we have, it could quickly shrink to nothing if we were told that a miracle of healing rested upon the strength of our belief. When the sun is warm upon our shoulders and the wind is at our back, faith rises within us with the dawn of a new day. But the sunlit vision of faith can quickly turn into a dark nightmare of doubt and despair when the storm clouds move in to hide the face of God.

In Christopher Fry's play *The Boy with a Cart*, the shepherd boy Cuthman is told that while he was out tending the sheep, his father had died at home. When he is tired, the boy charges God to watch his sheep while he sleeps. God never fails. Now the boy cries out in anguish, "Did I steal God away from my father to guard my sheep? How can I keep pace with a pain that comes in my head so fast?" The People of South England serving as a chorus chant:

> The thongs of the daylight are drawn and slack.
> The dew crawls down to earth like tears.
> Root and sky break
> And will not mend with prayers.
> Only the minutes fall and stack
> Like a rising drum
> Where, thin as a draught through the crack,
> Death has whistled home. . . .
>
> How is your faith now, Cuthman? . . .
> Is God still in the air
> Now that the sun is down?
> They are afraid in the city,
> Sleepless in the town.
> Cold on the roads,
> Desperate by the river.
> Can faith for long elude
> Prevailing fever?[1]

No wonder the disciples cried out to Jesus, "Increase our faith!" (Luke 17:5).

On another occasion he said to them, "Truly I tell you, if you have faith the size of a mustard seed, you will say to this mountain, 'Move from here to there,' and it will move; and nothing will be impossible for you" (Matt. 17:20). Realizing Jesus' penchant for metaphors, we probably should not use faith where bulldozers will do the job. But he does seem to suggest that faith is a means of dealing with what would otherwise be impossible.

It is not the quantity of faith that counts but the quality. Even a little faith, according to Jesus, is sufficient to produce miraculous results. Having even a small amount of faith we can do what seems impossible. Does this mean that if the mountain does not move we have no faith? Is the test of faith the result it produces? What difference does faith make; what is faith meant to accomplish in our lives?

Can faith overcome clinical depression; can it replace a lost love or repair a broken one? Aside from its religious value as a condition for receiving divine approval, does faith have any practical value for everyday life? Is faith only a psychological crutch meant to give us spiritual consolation when things don't work as we had hoped, or is faith meant to work when nothing else does?

We go to church to confess our faith in God. To be sure that the words are proper and not lacking in theological content, they are printed for us in the liturgy and sung in the creed. We should not be spontaneous at such a crucial moment. As Annie Dillard once wrote, "I often think of the set pieces of liturgy as certain words which people have successfully addressed to God without their getting killed."[2]

For all the holy terror of the sanctuary, a confession of faith, as some have discovered, is easier to make than the living out of faith. Facing life out in the world can sometimes be more difficult than facing God in the sanctuary.

Faith at work is apparently more pleasing to God than faith at rest. The profession of faith is fine, wrote James, but what good is it without works? "Even the demons believe," James reminded his readers. For James, faith that didn't work was of no practical value. While others made great claims to faith, James countered, "I by my works will show you my faith" (James 2:18–19). James appears to be giving us an early version of the more recent Twelve Step admonition that change will not occur until we "walk the talk."

The Vision of Faith

The person whose faith goes no farther than making a confession of faith in God does not attract our attention as much as one who lives out faith with vision and commitment. We admire the virtue of faith when its vision leads to victory in the struggle of life. The woman who suffered the loss of her children turned away from the gaping hole and rubble in which her children died to envision new life out of death.

Like Job of old, she proclaimed by her faith, "The LORD gave, and the LORD has taken away; blessed be the name of the LORD" (Job 1:21). In her vision of faith, she saw the faces of children yet unborn and embraced them with grief-stricken love and grace-filled hope. Her bruised and broken spirit touched the heart of God and received new life. Only one who has never struggled in desperate circumstances to proclaim God's blessed name, to embrace grief and bring a broken spirit to God would consider these words a platitude. This is faith at work.

Faith has a spiritual core that defies the logic of death and despair. Faith is the exception to the rule that something cannot come out of nothing. God created the world "out of nothing," and faith is the creative power of spirit that enlightens the void with vision and breaks the silence with singing. Those who demonstrate exceptional faith appear to have a vision that propels them into extraordinary action.

Such faith is a central theme in the Bible. It is a quality attributed to Noah when God told him to build the ark. It was by faith that Abraham was declared righteous and, along with Sarah, received the promise through which their family and all the families of the earth would be blessed (see Gen. 12). Hebrews 11 is devoted entirely to a recitation of those who were honored for their faith. "Without faith it is impossible to please God," the author of Hebrews warned (11:6).

Not only did Abraham leave his family and country to set out on a pilgrimage to a new land, he went out "not knowing where he was going" (Heb. 11:8). When he arrived in the land he understood to be his inheritance from God, he found that it was occupied by natives who were not about to move over and give title to him. No matter. "He looked to the city that has foundations" and lived as a nomad and pilgrim in the land promised to him. When he despaired of having a son, being "as good as dead," through faith he received a son from his barren wife when he was close to one hundred years old (11:12).

The faith of Abraham and Sarah was captured by a vision, passed on from one generation to another. They went out not knowing where they were going! Yet the call was to go forward, not back. The vision of faith is a direction even if it is not a road map. Their vision was compelling, though not at all times clear. There are times when we move forward in life more by what is compelling than by what is clear.

But here is where faith approaches the threshold of fanaticism. When put to the test, Abraham did not stumble in unbelief but agreed to offer up as a sacrifice his only son, Isaac, on Mt. Moriah in obedience to God. Only divine intervention prevented a murder, as if his willingness to commit the act was sufficient proof of his faith. Yet even in this terrible trial, Abraham's vision of God's creative power and promise sustained his faith: "He considered the fact that God is able even to raise someone from the dead—and figuratively speaking, he did receive him back" (Heb. 11:19).

We stand back with a mixture of awe and horror at such a test of faith. When we measure faith against doubt, only a terrible trial seems sufficient to purify and verify authentic faith. Abraham's vision of faith focused upon the Word of the Lord, and the same Lord who summoned forth his faith held him back from a fantastic and fanatical act. In the end, he discovered that the God in whom he believed was a God who demanded obedient love, not brutal sacrifice.

The narrative of Abraham's trial of faith searches out the hidden guilt that lurks in the spiritual core of every person. This primeval guilt fashions a god in our own image whose anger can only be propitiated with our pain and whose pleasure can only be satisfied with sacrifice. Human sacrifice to the gods is a common theme running through primitive human religion. With modern sensibilities more sophisticated, these sacrifices are not quick and bloody but perpetual and provisional. The god that guilt serves is never satisfied, and religious platitudes slide smoothly off the Teflon-coated surface of psychological anxiety. The human spirit can only be healed when it is broken, and applying religious palliatives to psychological guilt is spiritual malpractice.

Faith is a sign of spiritual fitness, without which we are condemned to fill the buckets in the religious prayer wheel with our own sweat and tears. In all cultures, mortifying the flesh in order to achieve spiritual virtue is a form of slavery, not sanctification.

Martin Luther triggered the Protestant Reformation with his discovery that we are justified before God by faith alone, apart from enslavement to our works. While that gave him freedom from a guilt-ridden drive to achieve salvation by his own efforts, it also splintered faith into a thousand sectarian versions, not a few of which have even led to bizarre manifestations including snake handling, self-mutilation, and, in some recent cases, mass ritual suicide.

The vision of faith is the open window of new and creative possibility, but when that vision goes out of focus, what was intended to be miraculous can become monstrous and mean. Fanatical faith is a faith whose vision has gone out of focus, leading to distortion and destruction.

Faith and folly are sibling rivals, growing up in the same household but not cut out of the same cloth. Folly may be likened to the weeds that grow amidst the wheat, appearing at early stages to be quite similar. It is only at harvest, said Jesus, that the wheat can be separated, when it has produced a full head of grain (see Matt. 13:24–30).

How then can we distinguish faith from folly? What are the evidences that we are cultivating true faith and not giving way to folly when we invest our lives in hopes and promises?

Finding the Clues to Keep Faith in Focus

Folly manufactures evidence where there is none, while faith sees evidence that is not visible. In retrospect, the difference becomes quite clear.

In a recent scandal where many Christians and Christian organizations lost millions of dollars in an investment scheme designed to double an organization's investment within six months, the basis for the promise was a group of "anonymous donors" who would match the money invested. As it turned out, there were no "anonymous donors," and the person who created the scheme has now been sentenced to a long prison term. In this case, those who invested and the person who invented the scheme collaborated on the manufacture of evidence. The equation combined both grandiose zeal to promote the Lord's work and pure greed.

Folly, as it turns out, has two step-sisters—grandiosity and greed. Grandiosity, psychologists tell us, is the illusion that one is greater than one really is, leading to delusions of self-importance and success. Greed, of course, is the insatiable desire to accumulate things for the sake of gaining power and security.

Folly then is the attempt to "make visible" what is unreal and so elicit commitment from others and give oneself permission to satisfy greed and grandiosity. Folly and faith, as I have said, are siblings living in the same household. Faith envisions what is real, though not visible, while folly makes visible what is unreal. We need to look more closely at this distinction to find our clues.

The evidences on which faith rests are not always visible, though they are real. The author of the Book of Hebrews defines faith as "the assurance of things hoped for, the conviction of things not seen" (Heb. 11:1). These two elements comprise the evidences on which faith rests. Things that are hoped for are clearly not visible until they materialize. And things not seen are, by definition, invisible though still things.

When two people exchange wedding vows, for example, there are things hoped for that are not yet on the horizon of their relationship but that they believe will come to pass. There are also things not seen in a tangible sense, yet clearly present and real at the occasion.

When we believe a promise someone gives us, we do so on the basis of evidences that are not always visible. Such qualities as trust, dependability, and even love are expressions of the spirit of another. It is by actions that we make the invisible intentions of our spirits visible. At the same time, actions alone are insufficient evidences on which to pledge our life to another. A promise is an intention that goes beyond what has already been demonstrated in action and creates the vision of things hoped for that are still to come.

Some have looked back through the ruins of a disastrous and destructive marriage and declared the venture to have been folly, not faith. Christian organizations have been deceived by promises of exorbitant and quick return on money invested, only to discover to their dismay and shame that the venture was folly, not faith. In retrospect, folly is easy to see. But looking ahead, what may appear at the time to be faith may well turn out to be folly.

What are the clues to authentic faith?

Faith, as a former professor taught me, is "the resting of the entire self in the sufficiency of the evidences." In saying this, he stressed the fact that it is not the *kind* of evidences that warrant faith but the *sufficiency*.

When empirical evidences are sufficient that an airplane can actually lift off the ground, I step aboard. When statistical evidences are sufficient that a certified surgeon has successfully performed the same kind of operation many times, I submit to his knife. When evidences of another person's moral and spiritual integrity are sufficient, I entrust my life to them through vows and promises. The kind of evidences in each of these cases is quite different; but in each case, the evidences must be sufficient for us to release the kind of commitment that faith entails.

There can never be absolute certainty, of course. But "assurance" and "conviction" are sufficient for trust and commitment in the everyday course of our lives. The value of this concept of faith is that it relates faith to every aspect of life, not just to a so-called "spiritual" realm where we abandon rationality and practicality.

I do not fly on airplanes that have bad safety records and whose pilots are known addicts. I do not allow surgeons who have a known history of malpractice suits to operate on me. I do not trust persons who have proven to be unreliable in the past.

In each of these cases, however, the evidences are more or less visible so that sufficiency can be determined. There are other dimensions of life where the evidences are not so visible. How does one determine sufficiency in these cases?

The spiritual dimension of faith is the capacity of the self to envision evidences that are present but not always visible. This leads to convictions that translate into actions. If I am not convinced that the evidences are sufficient, it would be folly to make the "leap of faith." The clues we need to look for in keeping faith in focus are largely within ourselves.

Think again of the case of the woman in Oklahoma who underwent surgery in an attempt to have more children after losing her only two. Psychologists might question the motivation for her action, searching for evidences that she has not dealt with her loss in a healthy way and is seeking to "replace" her loss rather than accept it. They might also be concerned that she somehow feels responsible for not preventing this horrible tragedy and is now seeking to atone for her guilt.

She attributes her actions and attitude to her faith in God. If so, her intention is to mend a broken spirit and manifest spiritual fitness. She may also need to seek help and guidance to work on resolving psychological factors that may not yet be apparent. In the end, the evidences for faith that remain largely invisible will become manifest. As it is, she has shown her faith by her attitude and actions in accordance with the counsel of James.

Can each of us achieve such faith when we put it to our own test? I believe so, and here are some suggestions.

Make God part of the equation. When Job suffered loss he blessed the name of the Lord and allowed that what had happened was not beyond God's knowledge and ultimate responsibility. Having faith in God allows God to have some responsibility in the matter. We cannot exempt God from the bad things that happen and then trust him for the good things.

When we relegate God to a specific corner of our lives, the rest of our lives is devoid of spiritual power. As a result, we suffer a spiritual deficit of faith where we need it the most. Only the Spirit of God can mend a broken spirit and give it new life. What breaks our spirit cannot heal our spirit. Lack of faith is due to a spirit that has been crushed by disappointment, despair, and disillusionment experienced in everyday life. What once we named as faith turns out to be folly deceived by sibling rivalry!

Give your spirit some breathing room. The human spirit is "God-breathed" and needs some room to breathe (Gen. 2:7). Lack of faith is due to spiritual suffocation—holding our breath in the spiritual vacuum of an anxiety-filled chamber of fear.

Faith begins with the healing and restoration of our broken and bruised spirit. An anguished spirit is closer to the spiritual core of faith than an anxious spirit. When we fill each day with anxiety over what might happen, we bruise our spirit with bad news about that which is nonexistent! Faith knows that one moment of pain, when something actually does happen, is better than a thousand days of anxiety waiting for some unknown that never takes place.

Create a pathway for God to come. Faith is not the bridge we build to get to God—that is folly!—but it is creating a path for God to come to us.

When John the Baptist announced the coming of Jesus as the Messiah, he remembered the prophecy of Isaiah and said: "[I am] the voice of one crying out in the wilderness: Prepare the way of the Lord, make his paths straight" (Matt. 3:3; Isa. 40:3).

Creating a pathway for God is the opposite of manufacturing evidence for ourselves. When the woman in Oklahoma determined that her own creative and reproductive powers were the key to her own healing and hope, she set out to "make the path straight" for the Lord to work in her life.

Each of us has some creative gift, though it may have long lain dormant, and even, as in the case of this woman, may have been severed at the source. The prayer to have God restore our creative gift so that we may use it to "make a straight path" will always be answered—this is the promise of Jesus. We can "move mountains" with a small amount of faith when it has the creative energy of God breathed into it.

One morning, this woman arose and looked out through the window of her soul and saw a vision of what God could create through her. Her anguished spirit brushed the face of God, and she revived. "Without faith in God I don't know how I could have lived through this loss to rebuild my life." A miracle of faith indeed!

Choose your own pathway and make it straight—the Lord is coming!

13

Hope

Being Optimistic without Being Unrealistic

Now hope that is seen is not hope. For who hopes for what is seen? But if we hope for what we do not see, we wait for it with patience.

Romans 8:24–25

Hope is the lodestar that keeps faith on course. Faith is the sail we raise in hopes of catching a friendly breeze bringing us at last to the safe harbor of our desires and dreams. Without hope, faith can lose its way, susceptible to the fickle winds of fortune and fate.

The author of the Book of Hebrews has in mind a slightly different metaphor but captures the same truth: "We have this hope, a sure and steadfast anchor of the soul, a hope that enters the inner shrine behind the curtain, where Jesus, a forerunner on our behalf, has entered, having become a high priest forever according to the order of Melchizedek" (Heb. 6:19–20).

The inspiration for our faith is poured into our hearts from the wellspring of hope. The apostle Paul assures us that "hope does not disappoint us, because God's love has been poured into our hearts through the Holy Spirit that has been given to us" (Rom. 5:5).

There is a kind of hope that does disappoint us. False hope is a siren song enticing faith to raise its sails when there is no wind, as many have learned to their sorrow. Often, when facing the loss of what we value the most, we "keep our hopes up" that some miraculous intervention will occur and grant us our heart's desire. When our hope is finally crushed by the unavoidable reality of life, the sails of our faith lie tattered and torn at our feet.

Sometimes even a true hope can falter and die. Following the crucifixion of Jesus, two of his disciples were leaving Jerusalem on the road to Emmaus, despondent and despairing. Encountered by the risen Lord himself, they failed to recognize him. When pressed for an explanation as to their attitude, they recounted the sad fact of his crucifixion and then added, "We had hoped that he was the one to redeem Israel" (Luke 24:21). When their hope died, their faith collapsed. Only when the reality of his living presence broke through did their faith come to life. The same Jesus whom they saw die was now truly alive and in their midst. The reality of his presence rekindled their hope.

When Jesus vanished from their sight, these two disciples followed the vision inspired by hope and hurried to their friends to bear witness to their newborn faith. The reality of his Spirit set them on a course that led into the future rather than retreated to the past.

Hoping against Hope

Hope is a spiritual virtue, and without it we cannot experience spiritual maturity or spiritual balance. "Hope that is seen is not hope," the apostle Paul reminds us. "But if we hope for what we do not see, we wait for it with patience" (Rom. 8:24–25).

True hope is a virtue that we admire in others and that we seek for ourselves. But if we cannot see that for which we hope, how then is it possible to distinguish the hope that does not fail from false hope, which may sustain us for a time but in the end has no reality?

As we trace out the contours of hope as a spiritual virtue, we will learn what the apostle meant when he said of Abraham: "Hoping against hope, he believed that he would become 'the father of many nations,' according to what was said" (Rom. 4:18). "Hoping against hope" is the reach of the human spirit for the promises of God as inspired by the Spirit of God.

Tracing the Virtue of Hope: The Spiritual Power of Discernment

Parents give children false hope when they promise a gift, a trip, or time and attention with no intention of fulfilling the promise or even an opportunity to do so. "I'll go out and play catch with you on Saturday," a father might say to his son in order to divert him from some immediate request for attention. When Saturday comes, the father may excuse himself from the promise by saying, "I'm sorry, son, but I have to take the car down to have it serviced today. It is the only day that I have time off from work."

The child's hopes are dashed, but he has no recourse. His father has a good reason not to keep his promise. It is a minor thing in the mind of the parent. Kids are always demanding something. But when this becomes a pattern, one learns not to count on promises made by those who are unable or unwilling to keep them. The lesson learned is: Don't hope for something you can't get for yourself.

A young girl who has always wanted to be a doctor prepares herself by taking a pre-med course in college. Alas, when it comes time to apply for medical school, her father dies, and she has to give up that dream in order to find employment to help support her mother and her younger brothers. Her hope of becoming a doctor was not unrealistic but, in the end, was not possible. Duty is a virtue that often drives a stake into the heart of hope.

In former times (and perhaps in some families today), a young woman started a "hope chest" by laying aside for her marriage items that were beautiful and useful, such as linens and silver. This quaint custom, by its very name, underscored the conviction that being a wife was more than a role; it was the realization of a young girl's dreams. Today, however, with the rising rate of domestic violence in marriage and the fact that one half of all marriages end in divorce, hope too often becomes an early casualty of failed love. I have not heard of hope chests for second marriages! And yet, people's willingness to enter marriage again is itself a testimony to hope.

In *After the Fall*, a play by Arthur Miller, Quentin surveys his life with a sad and cynical eye. He has two divorces in his safe deposit box, a failed relationship where he attempted to save a desperate woman from suicidal self-destruction by the power of love, and the ruins of a Nazi death camp to remind him of the murderous possibilities in the heart of otherwise normal people, including his own. He has met a German woman named Holga, a survivor of the collapse of a civilization into the ruins of war. Close to giving up all hope, Quentin ponders the mystery of her hope.

"That woman hopes!" he cries out. "Or is that exactly why she hopes, because she knows? What burning cities taught her and the death of love taught me: that we are very dangerous! And that, that's why I wake each morning like a boy—even now, even now! To know, and even happily, that we met unblessed; not in some garden of wax fruit and painted trees, that lie of Eden, but after, after the Fall, after many, many deaths. . . . No, it's not certainty. I don't feel that. But it does seem feasible . . . not to be afraid."[1]

Miller reminds us that the capacity to hope lies on this side of Eden, where perfection and innocence no longer exist. With the loss of idealism, true hope is born. When the hope chest, with its cherished dreams of perfect love, is just another item at the yard sale, new hope arises as the reach of the human spirit for that which is at least feasible, if no longer fantastic.

Hope springs eternal in the human heart, so says the sage. All things considered, that is certainly true. But not everyone survives the loss of innocence when it comes to hope. The rebirth of hope out of the ashes of failure, like the mythical *phoenix*, is glorious in its appearance. But for some the ashes remain cold and dark. We admire hope as a virtue in those who survive the death of hope and yet continue to hope. These are the ones, like Abraham, who "hope against hope."

There is something about hope that defies explanation, much like the human spirit itself. We all know people whose spirit refuses to give up, who, moved by some invisible force, have a vision of a future that gives them meaning and purpose for the present.

Allen is such a person. After a spinal cord injury from a motorcycle accident left him paraplegic, he saw his dream of becoming a professional athlete crash and burn. When suicidal thoughts crept in during the early weeks of his hospitalization, he battled them with a will to live a life that had no content or purpose. Without a means of making a living, he chose life. Without the means of caring for himself, he accepted care as a way of life. Drifting in the twilight zone of an ambiance that excused him from having to lift as much as a finger (literally!), he felt the air begin to move his wings (figuratively), and his spirit began to soar.

Having a nodding acquaintance with God through an untested and untroubled childhood faith, he began to get serious and directed some pointed questions to the invisible deity that lurked around the edges of his consciousness. "All right, God," he said one day. "You created the world out of nothing; let's see what you can do with me!"

In recounting this, Allen said that for the first time in his life, he viewed God as someone he could talk to without having to be sure of using the right words. "After all," he said, "what more could God do to me? If he didn't like it, he could just turn away and leave me alone. I was not in a position to cause him any trouble."

As it turned out, he didn't get any answer; no disembodied voice came to him with the cosmic vibes of a Charlton Heston. Nothing. But a strange stirring in his own spirit took place. "I felt like part of me had wings," he said, "and I was lifted by an invisible breath so that I could see my situation from a different perspective. I gained a vision for what I might do within the limitations of my physical disability and found a new hope for my life."

When he was released from the rehabilitation unit and able to use a wheelchair, he enrolled in a program leading to a doctorate in clinical psychology at a Christian school and is now a licensed therapist.

Recently, I asked him a purely theoretical question. "Allen, if you had a chance to go back and live that tragic moment over again, and escape the accident, retaining your original physical ability, would you choose to do that?"

"That is really hard to answer," he responded slowly. "But to do so would annihilate the person that I have now become. I had thought my identity was going to be found through my profession; now it is my possession. I have become all that I could have hoped for—what more can one ask of life?"

That is Allen's story. His spirit was moved, I believe, by the Spirit of God, and he gained the spiritual power of discernment. He had hoped to find fulfillment and satisfaction through attaining a boyhood dream. When he awoke, his life was a nightmare, and that hope died. What we see now in his life is the virtue of a hope that each person can attain through the gift of spiritual discernment of his or her own special mission and place in life.

While Allen's legs remain paralyzed, the wings of his spirit carry him farther than he ever dreamed possible. From his story I learned the meaning of the prophet's poetry: "Even youths will faint and be weary, and the young will fall exhausted; but those who wait for the LORD shall renew their strength, they shall mount up with wings like eagles, they shall run and not be weary, they shall walk and not faint" (Isa. 40:30–31).

The spiritual power of discernment leads to the birth of hope. Discernment is itself a gift of the Spirit, as the apostle said: "What no eye has seen, nor ear heard, nor the human heart conceived, what God has prepared for those who love him—these things God has revealed to us through the Spirit; for the Spirit searches everything, even the depths of God" (1 Cor. 2:9–10).

Spiritual discernment moves the wings of the soul and stirs the creative imagination of the heart. If hope springs eternal in the human heart, only those who plant the seeds reap the harvest.

Planting the Seeds of Hope: The Creative Power of Visualization

During the long winter months on the farm in South Dakota where I grew up, a favorite pastime for my parents was perusing the brightly colored seed catalogues that came in the mail. As they did this, they visualized the fruit, flowers, and vegetables they planned to grow the following summer.

The catalogues had no pictures of the seeds themselves but of the luscious fruit, blooming flowers, and colorful vegetables! While the metaphor of sowing seeds is a powerful one, it is the visualization of the harvest that stirs the imagination and inspires hope.

Planting seeds in the dark, damp soil in early spring is an exercise in hope, inspired by the vision of the harvest that the warm sunny days of summer will produce. The creative power of visualization that engenders hope as a future and invisible promise is captured by the human spirit as a component of present reality. Hope is a creative visualization produced through the imaginative power of the spirit.

We can only grasp the reality of the spirit through a certain type of "illusion," says Ernest Becker in his Pulitzer Prize winning book. Life-enhancing illusions, he wrote, are those which arouse faith and produce the character necessary to face adversity with courage and conviction. Such illusions do not lie, but produce authentic faith in the spiritual realities which are true and eternal.[2]

The use of visualization to create such "illusions" is common in the Bible. The psalmist envisions the Lord as a shepherd who guides the sheep to a place where there are "green pastures and still waters" that restore the soul. "You prepare a table before me in the presence of my enemies." The reader is stimulated to imagine the scene and to anticipate the blessing of "dwelling in the house of the Lord my whole life long" (Ps. 23).

Does such visualization work? In his book *Death Camp to Existentialism*, the Austrian psychiatrist Viktor Frankl, himself a survivor of Auschwitz, reported that those prisoners who visualized life beyond the concentration camp had a higher rate of survival than those who did not. He urged his fellow prisoners to imagine what it would be like to be released, to feast on their favorite food, to walk in the garden, to smell the flowers, and to be embraced by their loved ones. Those who did had a higher rate of survival on their meager diet under brutal conditions.[3]

Hope is visualizing the invisible promise.

Planting the seeds of hope follows visualization of the harvest. Without seeds, the harvest of hope is a true illusion—a lie of the imagination that can never bear fruit.

Not every sowing produces a harvest. The hope engendered during the winter is sometimes cruelly snatched away by a slashing summer storm. One such incident taught me a lesson about hope that I shall never forget.

It was Saturday evening and harvesttime. I was but a young boy, and I had to stretch my legs to match my father's stride as we walked out into the barley field. The ripening grain reached almost to my father's waist and to my shoulders as we waded into this river of gold. "It's about ready," my father said, as much to himself as to me. "Come Monday we will begin cutting."

I don't know what his dreams were that night, but mine were of the excitement of following the horse-drawn harvester around the field, watching the bundles spew out, each tied with rough twine by the clicking fingers of the mechanical apparatus. My job was to stack them into shocks with the grain ends on top, forming a bearded bouquet of sunlit straw.

But it was not to be. On Sunday afternoon, a thunderstorm marched across the prairie, stabbing the ground with lightning strokes and pelting all that lay within its glowering stride with a merciless pounding of hailstones. The frozen pellets of ice drove animals under cover, tore shingles off the roof, and cut the standing grain to a mangled mass of broken straw.

When the storm had passed, we walked once more out into the field. My father surveyed the sodden field with eyes as practiced in measuring chaos as in envisioning a harvest. When he spoke, it was directly to me, as though he were depositing the words, like seeds, into a freshly plowed field. "Son," he said, "when this field dries out, we will begin to work it to keep the weeds down. A fall rain is good for the subsoil. We still have seed for planting in the spring, and it will grow a better crop next year for all of this."

Misfortune had struck. And my father struck back in the only way he knew how. He wagered the power of the seed against the fury of the storm. By the time he had returned to the farmhouse that Sunday evening, he had decided which crop he would plant in that field! He had not lost hope, only a harvest. His thoughts were already on the coming spring and planting season.

We can only have strong feelings for that which has the capacity to break our hearts. We can only mend a broken heart by sowing the seeds for a future harvest. He loved the soil and the seed more than the harvest! This is the lesson hope teaches us.

In my youth, I was more fascinated with harvesttime than planting time. The drudgery of chores in the winter and the bleak days of early spring planting seldom stirred my soul. The care of the crops during the hot days of summer was a battle against weeds, insects, and worrisome weather. I had no positive feelings for these days and duties. My emotions were fixed on harvesttime!

I saw the barley harvest as the only thing that counted. When devastation struck, I had no comprehension that, for my father, this misfortune, though it caused hardship and personal disappointment, was not the collapse of his life investment in farming. Not only had he learned to diversify his crops so that the harvest season was spread out over a longer period, he had learned to diversify his emotional investment in life. No misfortune at harvesttime had the power to rob him of the self-fulfillment experienced at planting time! He struck back by launching another season of planning.

There is spiritual wisdom and personal power in taking the initiative in the face of life's misfortunes. Life teaches us that spiritual fitness results from emotional diversity.

Not every seed will produce a harvest, but the planting of seeds is a step of faith that renews hope.

Bearing the Burden of Hope: The Practical Power of Faith

There are dreamers in life, and then there are doers. We call the dreamers impractical and tolerate their fantasies with the indulgence granted to the young and immature. "If wishes were horses, all beggars would ride," my mother used to say when I expressed my desires by saying, "I wish I had . . ." or "I wish I could . . ." As I grew up I discovered that translating my wishes into reality was part of the practical power of faith. But this often required "bearing the burden of the seed."

The Hebrew psalmist put this philosophy of life in poetic form.

> May those who sow in tears
> reap with shouts of joy.
> Those who go out weeping,
> bearing the seed for sowing,
> shall come home with shouts of joy,
> carrying their sheaves.
> Psalm 126:5–6

A literal translation of the Hebrew reads this way:

> He surely toils along weeping,
> carrying the burden of seed;
> he surely comes in with rejoicing,
> carrying his sheaves.

The burden of hope can only be borne through the practical power of faith. Let me suggest two ways in which faith carries the burden of hope.

First, the burden of hope is the anguish over what has already been lost. In the poignant sonnet by Edna St. Vincent Millay, it is with "twisted face" that the man with the pocket full of seeds moves toward the future. We should never forget this. The burden of hope always emerges out of the ruins of some failed dream, some unfulfilled desire, some loss that must be grieved.

> The broken dike, the levee washed away,
> The good fields flooded and the cattle drowned,
> Estranged and treacherous all the faithful ground,
> And nothing left but bloating disarray
> Of tree and home uprooted . . . was this the day
> Man dropped upon his shadow without a sound
> And died, having laboured well and having found
> His burden heavier than a quilt of clay?
> No, no, I saw him when the sun had set
> In water, leaning on his single oar
> Above his garden faintly glimmering yet . . .
> There bulked the plough, here washed the updrifted
>   weeds . . .
> And scull across his roof and make for shore,
> With twisted face and pocket full of seeds.[4]

There is a kind of hope that carries no burden. But it is childish and immature. It is short-term and short-lived. It flickers brightly for an instant and then just as quickly dissolves with the first tears of frustration over the loss of some simple pleasure. Hope is not a wish or desire that can be washed away with the first summer storm. That hope is merely a fantasy of the mind, a lying illusion that shares the same bed with fear—both are ghosts in the night and cannot survive the bright light of day.

Hope requires risk, so much that it hurts. Hope makes us vulnerable to future, even greater, loss. Hope exposes us to disappointment, frustration, and betrayal. Faith plants the seed and promises a harvest, and so creates hope.

But with the promise of a harvest comes the possibility that the promise will fail. That is the betrayal that hope must bear. Without faith as the investment of one's precious life and resources in the power of life, the burden of hope could not be borne. But faith bears that burden in partnership with hope, for it is partnership with God, the author and creator of life.

Second, the burden of hope is the responsibility that attends the bearer of the seed. The one who bears the seed is not just a carrier, but a sower! Seed can be borne in a bucket and stowed in a sack. The burden of the seed is the responsibility that lies upon the sower to prepare the soil and to nurture the growth of the seed through to harvest.

The burden of hope bears the responsibility for taking up life again when there has been foolishness and failure. The story of the prodigal son is not the story of one who comes home to negotiate a better deal but of the restoration of a son who had squandered his inheritance (Luke 15). When the boy wanted to come home to be a servant, the father said, in effect, "No, you will be a sower and not a servant" and gave him a "pocket full of seeds"! That was his burden. Only a son can become a prodigal. He did not dare hope for so much, but when he was restored, along with the restoration came the burden of hope and seeds to sow.

When a woman was brought before Jesus disgraced and condemned for her sin of adultery, Jesus told her that he did not condemn her. "Go your way, and from now on do not sin again" (John 8:11). Her forgiveness and freedom also became the burden of hope. She went away with "twisted face and pocket full of seeds," bearing more responsibility as a result than she ever had under the law! She now had a life of partnership with God, which, through faith, would enable her to bear the burden of responsibility. This responsibility is not only to sow the seed but to carry the hope of others whose livelihood depends upon the harvest.

To be a sower one must not only accept the yoke of life and enter into partnership with the creative power of God but must also, in the process, engender the trust of others. In the pocket of the sower are not only the seeds of a future crop but the hopes of all who depend upon the harvest that is promised.

The burden of hope is the burden of carrying the responsibility for the hope of others, even when they have no faith. When Jesus set out to go to Jerusalem for what would be the last time, his disciples pleaded with him not to go. Peter, in fact, "took [Jesus] aside and began to rebuke him. But turning and looking at his disciples, he rebuked Peter and said, 'Get behind me, Satan! For you are setting your mind not on divine things but on human things'" (Mark 8:32–33).

The destiny of the disciples rested upon Jesus' commitment to follow to the end the path he had chosen in obedience to his Father in heaven. What moved Jesus to bear the burden of the seed in the face of the fear and fatalism of his disciples? The author of the Book of Hebrews tells us that Jesus is the pioneer and perfecter of our faith, "who for the sake of the joy that was set before him endured the cross, disregarding its shame, and has taken his seat at the right hand of the throne of God" (Heb. 12:2).

His faith enabled him to invest that which was most precious to him—his own life and the lives of all who followed him—in the future God had prepared. His burden of hope was not only the responsibility for taking up the way of his own cross but also his obligation to take care of all who trusted and followed him.

The gift of faith is not the burden. Rather, faith is God's empowering us to bear the burden of hope and to sow and tend the seed. This seed is an investment of something precious to us in utter dependence upon the promise of a harvest through a power over which we have no control. Our hope, finally, is in God, not in the harvest of our own ambition. When we open the window of hope to the power of God's love, we find healing for our hurts and hope for our hearts.

Opening the Window of Hope: The Healing Power of Love

The apostle Paul reminds us that the created world was subjected to futility *in hope* that creation itself would be set free from bondage to decay and obtain the freedom of the glory of the children of God (see Rom. 8:19–21). There is a window of hope in every wall that closes in upon us. There is a promise of healing for every hurt and a measure of grace poured into every grief. God has made it so. Hope is not the sun that never sets but a morning star in the darkest and longest night.

Not every rainfall will produce a flood, nor will every cloud produce rain! Not every sickness leads to a death, but death does occur, senseless and outrageous to the human spirit. Having lost one child, can we bear the burden of hope and risk having and possibly losing another one? Will the burden of anguish and responsibility be too much? How will one survive through the inevitable childhood sicknesses that follow the birth of every child, when such sickness has already produced one death?

Hope was first expressed in the Bible following the first murder. Eve was the mother of two sons, Cain and Abel. When Cain killed Abel, we read, "Adam knew his wife again, and she bore a son and named him Seth, for she said, 'God has appointed for me another child instead of Abel, because Cain killed him'" (Gen. 4:25). I can hear her whisper to herself, "Will Cain slay him? Will I lose this son too?"

Not all jealousy and hatred leads to murder. But murders and violence do occur. Eve has chosen to have another child. There will be jealousy and anger again; can one bear the burden of helplessness in the face of such uncertainty?

Having been betrayed once, will one dare to trust again? Not every plot that develops in human relationships becomes a betrayal. But is there any real relationship without the subplots that have the power to destroy what love has created?

There are those who would not have risked another child, another tragic loss. There are those who prefer never to try again rather than to suffer the anguish of bearing hope.

With poetic pathos, Anne Morrow Lindbergh bares her own grief and shares her vision of the power of love to give new birth to hope.

> For whom
> The milk ungiven in the breast
> When the child is gone?
>
> For whom
> The love locked up in the heart
> That is left alone?
>
> That golden yield
> Split sod once, overflowed an August field,
> Threshed out in pain upon September's floor,
> Now hoarded high in barns, a sterile store.
>
> Break down the bolted door;
> Rip open, spread and pour
> The grain upon the barren ground
> Wherever crack in clod is found.
>
> There is no harvest for the heart alone;
> The seed of love must be
> Eternally
> Resown.[5]

The power of the seed is its capacity to draw what it needs from the limitless resources around it, provided that it is sown! This is why the metaphor of sowing is such an apt one for the discovery of hope. Though our faith be as small as a mustard seed, Jesus reminded us, it can move mountains (see Matt. 17:20). This is not because of the power that resides in the seed, for it is helpless until it is sown. The power comes from the source upon which faith draws. When our hope is in God, we draw upon his limitless love as the source of our faith.

The seed of hope is love, and, as Anne Lindbergh tells us, it must be eternally resown. But there are bolted doors to break down and windows to open in our soul before we can harvest hope from the sowing of love. "Rip open, spread and pour the grain upon the barren ground wherever crack in clod is found." Lord, give us the seed of love that we may lavish it upon our barren ground.

14

Love

Going the Second Mile without Going out of Bounds

Love is patient; love is kind; love is not envious or boastful or arrogant or rude. It does not insist on its own way; it is not irritable or resentful; it does not rejoice in wrongdoing, but rejoices in the truth. It bears all things, believes all things, hopes all things, endures all things. Love never ends.

1 Corinthians 13:4–8

We are not born with the virtue of love. We are born with appetites and instincts. We emerge from the womb equipped to reach out for what we want but not prepared to give what others need. Only when love shines upon us from the face and touch of others does our capacity for love stir from its natal sleep and awaken in response.

To be born with blue eyes is not a virtue (I must confess!), nor are color of skin and other ethnic indicators marks of character. What we admire in others as a virtue is a quality of life that they have achieved, not what they have inherited.

That we are capable of love is evidenced by the fact that we can respond to love when it is given. The smile of a baby, the rush of a toddler into loving arms, the tears of a two-year-old when left with a baby-sitter entreat love to stay. Oh, it is true! We are born with a vacuum that only love can fill!

But to actually give love is a virtue that must be learned, a grace that must be acquired. The same child that finds comfort in being loved can be quite oblivious to the needs of a parent and downright cruel in denying love to a sibling when struggling for possession of a favorite toy. When our children surprise us with spontaneous acts of caring and giving, we are amazed and pleased at these early signs of what we hope will become a character trait.

The essence of virtue and the quintessence of character are the possession and expression of love. A truly loving person is like a rare gem discovered amidst the colored beads and costume jewelry in the tray at every garage sale. Though we ourselves are amateurs at loving, we have the eye of an expert when it comes to spotting the real thing. But unlike a flawless diamond, love is valuable not because it is rare but because it is real. If every person had the virtue of love, it would still be a virtue that we would admire and cherish. For the virtue of love is that it makes the common uncommon, the routine ritual a royal ceremony, and the simplest service a sacramental grace.

One who loves creates a reality that would otherwise not exist and sustains a value that would otherwise be lost. The reality that love cherishes is fragile, for it could not exist except for the love that created and upholds it. At the same time, no other power can destroy what love cherishes, for love is also fierce and strong.

The Hebrew poet sings of such a love: "Set me as a seal upon your heart, as a seal upon your arm; for love is strong as death, passion fierce as the grave. Its flashes are flashes of fire, a raging flame. Many waters cannot quench love, neither can floods drown it" (Song of Sol. 8:6–7).

Love is a virtue because it demonstrates patience rather than petulance, responds with kindness when confronted by the failures of others, and goes out of its way to contribute to the needs of others, even at its own expense. As the apostle Paul said in concluding his hymn in praise of love, "It bears all things, believes all things, hopes all things, endures all things. Love never ends" (1 Cor. 13:7–8).

"How do I love thee?" wrote Elizabeth Barrett Browning. "Let me count the ways."

> I love thee to the depth and breadth and height
> My soul can reach, when feeling out of sight
> For the ends of Being and ideal Grace.
> I love thee to the level of everyday's
> Most quiet need, by sun and candle-light.
> I love thee freely, as men strive for Right;
> I love thee purely, as they turn from Praise.
> I love thee with the passion put to use
> In my old griefs, and my childhood's faith.
> I love thee with a love I seemed to lose
> With my lost saints,—I love thee with the breath,
> Smiles, tears, of all my life!—and, if God choose,
> I shall but love thee better after death.[1]

Love within Bounds

The virtue of love, Jesus taught, is not only that we love those who love us but that we love those who are not easy to love and who will need more than we are prepared to give. Love must be willing to "go . . . the second mile" (Matt. 5:41). But what about the third or fourth mile? How far can love go without going out of bounds?

"I tried to love my husband and children as the Bible said I should," Julie told her pastor. "I served their every need and even their whims. I accepted their complaints and criticisms without answering back. I practically wore myself out trying to practice this kind of love and ended up being nothing more than a doormat for them to walk on."

Julie tried to bear all things, hope all things, and endure all things. She turned the other cheek, gave up her cloak as well as her coat, and went far beyond the second mile! But in the end "things" sucked the life out of her soul and left her spiritually and emotionally devastated. She is to be pitied, not admired. There is no virtue in being a doormat and letting others walk all over you. But she did her best to give what she thought was love. What went wrong?

My friend and colleague Lewis Smedes gives us a clue in his book *Love within Limits.* He suggests that healthy love is realistic and does not pander to the capricious and unbridled needs of others to suck up all of our love. There are lines to be drawn, says Smedes, when we say "enough!"[2] Love bears all things and endures all things, wrote the apostle. But only if it is true love and not the neurotic need to bear everyone else's cross and endure suffering with a martyr's passion for self-immolation.

Love is not defined by *what* it endures but *that* it endures. Love is not the sacrifice of the self to an ideal, like a light-starved moth flying into the floodlight until its eyes are blinded, its wings scorched, and its body burned to a crisp. No. Love is a creative partnership that stays within bounds in order that each might expand the boundaries of a self-contained life.

To say that love is realistic is to acknowledge the fact that our need to give in the name of love may be a concealed attempt at self-gratification. When we are starved for love, it sometimes happens that we rob our pantry of bread and milk to give to others in hopes of getting cake and ice cream in return. Julie thought that she was giving love. In fact, she was providing maid service to her family and sexual favors to her husband in hopes of getting back some love. Prostitutes are more realistic. When they turn a trick, they get their money in advance and look for love elsewhere. Knowing what love is not (or knowing the limits of love) is the first step toward learning to love.

Let us look at some of the boundaries that define love as a virtue and as a mark of spiritual fitness.

The Boundary of Positive Effect

Jesus sent his disciples out with a message of God's love, with the purpose of providing healing and hope. He gave them instructions that included the limits of love and clear boundaries. "Whatever town or village you enter, find out who in it is worthy, and stay there until you leave. As you enter the house, greet it. If the house is worthy, let your peace come upon it; but if it is not worthy, let your peace return to you. If anyone will not welcome you or listen to your words, shake off the dust from your feet as you leave that house or town" (Matt. 10:11–14).

"If the house is not worthy," Jesus said, "let your peace return to you." To go farther would be to go out of bounds. Those deemed unworthy were those who did not receive the gift of peace and love as it was intended. God's love is measured by the positive effect it is intended to produce. Where love does not create its intended effect, it has reached its limit.

What Julie had not learned was to measure her love by the positive effect it created in her children and husband. Starved for love, she sought it in the only way she knew— attending to the needs of others in hopes of receiving some attention. Instead of irrigating a field in order that it become productive and fruitful, her love flowed directly into the ditch that drained into a swamp. Instead of enriching and building up the lives of those she loved, she allowed them to sink deeper into the mire of self-indulgence.

Attached by the cords of compulsive care, she was being drawn in after them. Helpless and hopeless, she could only cry out for help. In attempting to be a savior of others by self-sacrifice, she herself needed to be saved. She became a victim of the "lie of limitless love."

In Arthur Miller's play *After the Fall,* Quentin struggles to understand why his love could not save Maggie from her own willful self-destruction.

"If there is love," he cries out, "it must be limitless; a love not even of persons but blind, blind to insult, blind to the spear in the flesh, like justice, blind. . . ." In the end, he realizes that his love was really an attempt to exercise power, to be the savior of others. "God's power is love without limit. But when a man dares reach for that . . . he is only reaching for the power. Whoever goes to save another person with the lie of limitless love throws a shadow on the face of God."[3]

Love seeks the empowerment of others as a positive effect, not power over them. When we take on someone as a project in order that we become their savior, we contribute to their weakness as a way of gaining power. We may think that we have gone the second mile, but we have gone out of bounds.

The Boundary of Purposeful Passion

Love is not a torrent of water unleashed down the side of a mountain but a flow of water through a channel that irrigates a field. The river that graces the land with life-sustaining water becomes a devastating and destructive force when it overflows its boundaries. What makes a river is not the passivity of its current but the fact that its passion is kept within bounds.

Love without passion is anemic and sterile. The famous Dead Sea in Palestine is so called because it has no outlet. Eventually the salts and minerals in the water make it inhospitable for living organisms. When love dies and loses its passion it not only becomes sterile but toxic.

The love of God is portrayed by God's passionate anger as well as by his solicitous and searching care. The passionate lover is a fierce warrior who has righteous anger at that which demeans or destroys the object of love. But the passion in that anger is well aimed and not merely well armed. Its aim is accurate and its focus is narrow and laser-like in its clean and cutting edge.

Where the passion of love is without the boundary of purpose it becomes indiscriminate, promiscuous, and fatal. The passion of love can produce giddiness as well as gladness. Love that rides the crest of passion's wave becomes merely "high surf," and we must remember that waves only reach their crest when they are about to crash on shore.

Love is purposeful as well as playful. Love has expectations as well as excitement. Love is cautious as well as capricious. Love is creative and not chaotic. When those who love do not find a response, love has reached its limit. Yet love never exhausts its creative power and purpose. Love never ends.

The Boundary of Realistic Expectations

To say that love never ends is not to say that it is willing to be stretched to the breaking point, but that it has a reserve that is never exhausted. Julie lacked a realistic criterion by which she could keep her love within bounds. She had not learned to attach realistic expectations to her love in terms of the recognition and response of those she served in the name of love. When asked what she expected her love would produce in the lives of her children and her husband, she had no answer. "I thought that we were expected to show love without regard for any benefit to us," she finally said. "Isn't this the kind of love that God shows to us?"

She was partly correct, of course. God's love is given freely, with no strings attached. God does not love as a means of satisfying his own needs. At the same time, God's love is creative and purposeful, intended to benefit those whom he loves and to bring him pleasure.

God's love has clear expectations that are realistic as well as purposeful. God's love is not a rushing torrent that devastates all in its path. Nor is God's love naive and idealistic, blind to the realities and complexities of life. Like God's love, human love is realistic and resourceful, but it has its practical limits. One does not "simply" love and expect everything to work out. That is simplistic sentimentality.

The love that God expresses can be tough as well as tender. The prophet envisions the servant of the Lord as expressing God's love firmly but gently: "He will not cry or lift up his voice, or make it heard in the street; a bruised reed he will not break, and a dimly burning wick he will not quench; he will faithfully bring forth justice. He will not grow faint or be crushed until he has established justice in the earth" (Isa. 42:2–4).

Tough love is not brutal and unfeeling. Its toughness is not the absence of tenderness but the practical realism of its expectations. Love has realistic expectations regarding the yield on its investment. It also sets realistic criteria for measuring the goals it attempts to produce. The portfolio of love is set for high yield but low risk. The personal investment is total, but the expectations are in proportion to the growth potential.

Unrealistic expectations are the source of much disappointment and a great deal of pain in love. This is especially true when we conceal our expectations as a way of testing whether the other's love is spontaneous and creative. To expect a gift or an act of love from someone without giving clues to our expectations is to set the other person up for failure—unless they are lucky enough to have guessed right!

When our expectations are not met, it is usually because we expected the other person to do something for us or give something to us. Expectations cannot be realistic when we impose them upon others only to find the fulfillment of our own ideals.

Realistic expectations in love work in two ways. First, we cannot expect our love to control, manipulate, or coerce others. That is unrealistic. What is realistic is that through love we can present to others the mystery, uniqueness, and gift of creative partnership and companionship. We can do no more than that. To attempt to do more than that is to go out of bounds.

Second, we cannot place our own expectations upon others as an ultimatum or condition for accepting their love. What is realistic is to respect the boundary of the other person's freedom to be unique and creative in forming a partnership of reciprocity. When love is realistic it promotes freedom within which reciprocity enlarges and expands the boundaries of self-containment. Until love is able to grant the freedom of the other to be really free, true reciprocity and creative partnership and companionship cannot grow. The freedom of the other person is a border we cannot transgress without going out of bounds.

Anne Morrow Lindbergh captures this truth with poetic passion when she writes:

> Him that I love, I wish to be
> Free—
> Even from me.[4]

The Boundary of Creative Reciprocity

Learning to love is to learn the creative rule of reciprocity. The idea that altruism is the highest form of love is not a biblical truth. To love for the simple purpose of loving without regard for the creative effect of the love on both the one who gives and the one who receives is idealistic and not realistic. Such love easily goes out of bounds and quickly comes to an end.

Julie had this concept of love when she told her pastor that she understood the Bible to teach that one should love by serving others without regard for their response. The result was that her love went out of bounds. She was exploited by her own family, who took advantage of her without caring for her needs.

Julie may have spiritualized love by thinking of love as a sacrificial offering of herself upon the altar of marital duty and familial service. But there is no concept of reciprocity in sacrifice, for something must die in order that the gift upon the altar be purified of all self-interest.

Love devoid of all self-interest tends to obscure the personal aspect of the transaction in favor of the act itself. The spiritual aspect of love thus becomes less human for the sake of it registering on the divine scale. But when love becomes less human it does not become more divine and spirit filled, it simply becomes inhuman and spiritless.

Love, human love, love between persons, is a gift of the Spirit, and to love authentically, realistically, and effectively is to manifest spiritual fitness. Creative reciprocity is the boundary between human and inhuman love, between spirit-filled love and spiritless love. When we move beyond this boundary, we are out of bounds.

Where there is no creative reciprocity in a relationship, there is no creative partnership. Paradoxically, the boundaries of self-containment draw tighter even as the self attempts to pour out love without limits. The boundaries of Julie's true self were not expanded. She has become diminished and emaciated, more starved for love than ever. Seeking a more spiritual form of love by loving without regard to the diminishing return to her own spirit, Julie was slowly committing spiritual suicide. Her spiritual deprivation produced psychological despair and trauma to her physical well-being.

When love goes beyond the boundaries of positive effect, purposeful passion, realistic expectations, and creative reciprocity, it goes out of bounds. When love has no goal beyond the use of another as an object on which to expend its passion, it has gone out of bounds.

When the object of love is manipulated, exploited, and disempowered, it is a pretense of love, not authentic love. When the person who loves is used to gratify the self-indulgence of others, it is the abuse of love, not true love. "Going the second mile" may be "one mile too far"! The limit by which love operates is not the mile marker, but the goalpost. Without having a goal, love will always be a game played by losers.

But is creative reciprocity actually a biblical and spiritual truth?

The creative rule of reciprocity is clearly expressed by Jesus when he taught, "Forgive, and you will be forgiven; give, and it will be given to you. A good measure, pressed down, shaken together, running over, will be put into your lap; for the measure you give will be the measure you get back" (Luke 6:37–38).

"Through love become slaves to one another," wrote Paul (Gal. 5:13). "If we live by the Spirit, let us also be guided by the Spirit . . . for you reap whatever you sow" (5:25; 6:7). The law of sowing and reaping is the rule of creative reciprocity, it is the core of true spiritual balance.

"God's love has been poured into our hearts through the Holy Spirit that has been given to us" (Rom. 5:5). "We love because he first loved us" (1 John 4:19). There it is! The fruit of God's love is human love, a creative response of reciprocity.

Love is the jewel in the crown of virtues that belongs to those who seek and find the joys of balanced spirituality. "Pursue love and strive for the spiritual gifts," urges Paul (1 Cor. 14:1).

Love never ends, it is never finished, it never speaks the last word, it never reaches a conclusion that is not also a beginning.

And so . . . let us begin!

Notes

Chapter 1: Self-Control

1. George Gordon Byron, "Childe Harold's Pilgrimmage," canto 4, no. X. *The Complete Poetical Works of Lord Byron*, Cambridge edition (Boston: Houghton Mifflin, 1905).

Chapter 4: Compassion

1. Dietrich Bonhoeffer, *Ethics* (New York: Collins, 1970), 245–46.

Chapter 7: Wisdom

1. Anne Morrow Lindbergh, "Even," in *The Unicorn and Other Poems, 1935–55* (New York: Pantheon, 1956), 14.

Chapter 8: Honesty

1. Bonhoeffer, *Ethics*, 64–65.

Chapter 12: Faith

1. Christopher Fry, *A Boy with a Cart* (New York: Oxford University Press, 1959), 7–8.
2. Annie Dillard, *Holy the Firm* (San Francisco: Harper and Row, 1977), 59.

Chapter 13: Hope

1. Arthur Miller, *After the Fall* (New York: The Viking Press, 1972), 113–14.
2. Ernest Becker, *The Denial of Death* (New York: Macmillan, 1973), 158, 202.

Notes

3. Viktor Frankl, *Man's Search for Meaning: An Introduction to Logotherapy*, rev. ed., trans. Ilse Lasch (Boston: Beacon Press, 1963).

4. Edna St. Vincent Millay, "Wine from these Grapes," sonnet 10, in *Collected Poems*, ed. Norman Millay (New York: Harper and Row, 1956), 710.

5. Anne Morrow Lindbergh, "Second Sowing," in *The Unicorn and Other Poems, 1935–55* (New York: Pantheon Books, 1956), 32.

Chapter 14: Love

1. Elizabeth Barrett Browning, *Sonnets from the Portuguese* (Mount Vernon, NY: Peter Pauper Press, 1935), 54.

2. Lewis Smedes, *Love within Limits* (Grand Rapids: Eerdmans, 1978).

3. Miller, *After the Fall* (New York: The Viking Press, 1972), 106–7.

4. Anne Morrow Lindbergh, "Even," in *The Unicorn and Other Poems*, 13–14.

186

Index

Index